To

Frank

Wishing you True Wealth.

# Seasons of Wealth

*Parminder Bains*

First Published in Great Britain in 2019 by Springtime Books



ISBN: 978-1-9993040-2-7

Cover and internal pages designed by Catherine Brew
www.drawntoastory.com

**Health warning!**
Tax rules and allowances can and do change. This book does not provide formal advice. Some of the solutions have been simplified to demonstrate, in plain English, the outcomes for clients. There are a wide range of other stories and solutions, but their scope is beyond this book.

No action should be taken or inferred based on the contents of this book. You should seek professional advice from an independent Chartered Financial Planner or estate planning expert.

In many cases names have been changed.

All proceeds from the sale of this book go to the Seasons of Wealth Foundation to help cure those living with needless blindness in the world.

For my clients and their families who have changed the way I see the world forever.

# CONTENTS

*"There is no season such delight can bring, As Summer, Autumn, Winter, and the Spring."*

*William Browne*

# FOREWORD

Parminder Bains arrived in my life just as I was feeling ready to change direction. After 32 years of nurturing and running a business, the time seemed right to hand over the reins and embark on a new phase in life. I knew what I wanted to do. My two big questions were, "Could I afford it?" and "How could I make it happen?" Parminder shone a bright light on what I needed to consider as I embarked on a new career.

Preparations are in place for me to leave my organisation in a good position and in safe hands. In preparation for my second career, I'm now trained to teach qigong, a movement and breathing therapy, very important to those in stressful environments. I'm retaking my anatomy and physiology theory as a refresher before I do courses in acupressure and sacral cranial therapy. I'm planning to write a fantasy novel with my son, hopefully from a sunny place and to set up a mentoring consultancy of leaders and teachers in education and special needs.

I was very grateful to have someone to talk to as I leapt into action to create what could loosely be called "my bucket list". Having been introduced to Parminder by my accountant, I was looking forward to a fairly straightforward discussion about money.

What I got, was a great surprise. Parminder challenged me and not many people have ever done that before. He asked me some tough questions that deep down I'd been avoiding for far too long.

Through our conversations I discovered that the money wasn't the most important thing. It was me. Money was just a tool to help me live the life I wanted to live.

Through the Seasons of Wealth journey, with Parminder as my guide, I discovered some great things about myself. Most of the answers I sought were there all the time. They just needed teasing out. I gained great clarity about how my finances could be used and I made a meaningful connection between my life and my financial position.

Whatever 'Seasons of Life' you may be in and whatever your financial goals, this beautiful book will help you question and think and define your relationship with money. It will help you really focus on the things you can control, rather than those you can't, and put you on a firm path through your financial life, nurturing and tending to the important bits as you go.

I urge you to take on board Parminder's wisdom to help you achieve the life you want to lead.

*Dr Caroline Allen, OBE*
*CEO*
*Orchard Hill College Academy Trust,*
*Sutton, Surrey*

# ABOUT THIS BOOK

You have in your hands a book you can write, draw or doodle on. Go ahead and make it your own. Use it as a place where you can ponder and use your creativity to release some of your thoughts. A place where you sketch out your thoughts about your Seasons of Life and Wealth, about what's happened, happening or going to happen to you at each stage of your life.

As you journey through this book and the Seasons of Wealth, Life and Nature as I present them to you, I invite you to go and sit somewhere quiet to ponder and reflect. I have a magnificent twenty-foot maple tree in my back garden on the edge of my patio. When the weather is dry, I love to sit in its shade and think.

At the end of each chapter you will find the words Join Me Under the Maple Tree followed by what I consider to be tough love questions. These are the kinds of questions I ask my clients all the time during our many conversations. Usually they squirm a little, clear their throats and stare at the ceiling for a while before they answer. I know I'm putting them on the spot but I also know that these questions are in their best interests. These sections in my book will help you to look closely at your financial landscape and gain some clarity of thought along the way.

In each chapter I also introduce you to some of my clients because I hope their stories will help to illustrate some important facts. In the sections I call Meet the Clients you will learn about people like Jim, who wanted his wealth to remain with his direct descendants.

Consider this little book to be your own portable Financial Planner. It will share things with you that I share with my clients and, like them, you will have to get a little uncomfortable before you can move towards the ultimate goal of True Wealth.

Let me share with you my thoughts on the parallels between the Seasons of Nature, Life and Wealth. Join me as I share what I have learned about the meaning of True Wealth and how you too can move from Success to Significance.

*Parminder Bains*

*Seasons of Wealth*
*Summer 2019*

# HOW TO READ THIS BOOK

There is no point in telling Mother Nature what to do. She will do what she wants when she wants. Likewise, I am not going to tell you how to read this book either. All the same, I would like to take the liberty of recommending that you start with the Introduction and read through the chapters in order until you reach the end of the book to get a general overview. Take some time to reflect and then go back and read the Seasons that are most appropriate for you right now. Do this slowly, giving yourself a chunk of time away from interruptions so you can read, reflect and go through the exercise at the end of each chapter.

## So, what's Nature got to do with it?

This book uses the metaphor of Nature to describe the stages of our lives, our young adulthood, mid-life, retirement and then later life. Everyone gets started on their careers at a slightly different time, some in their 20s, some in their 30s, but some may enter working life in their teens. Similarly, while many people start their families and buy houses in their late 20s and 30s, some do so much later or much earlier and those who marry more than once may have more than one family. It is not for me to state emphatically that Spring is for people in their 20s, Summer for those in their 30s and 40s and that

Autumn begins when you turn 50. Retirement too, may begin when you are as young as 40 or as old as 75 even.

But know this – Spring, Summer, Autumn and Winter will occur in that order. You will move from one Season to the other at whatever age is right for you.

Consider the Seasons in this book to have flexible start and end dates and decide for yourself where you think you are right now.

Depending on which Season of Life you are in you may be tempted to turn to that Season in this book first. However, I have included all Seasons so that you can plan for both now and the future. If you are joining us in mid or later life, then you may benefit from looking back and reflecting on how you handled your finances. You may even be inspired by what you read to educate and prepare your children or grandchildren for their own financial future.

## This is what you can expect

Here's a brief outline of what we are going to cover in each of the chapters. Read this so you can decide which section or sections are going to be most important to you.

## PART ONE - SEASONS OF WEALTH

### Spring

You will be starting out with your career, family and home.

In this chapter I teach you about:

- ***Spring is for planting***
- When and why you should start saving
- The power of compound interest
- The spend, save, give principle
- How young John made the money for his first house.

### Summer

You will have established your career, family and home and may even be in a position to start doing something interesting with your money.

In this chapter I teach you about:

- ***Summer is for maintaining***
- How to nurture and sustain your savings and investments
- How to get your 'financial house' in order
- Why you need to make sacrifices
- How 38-year-old Paul consolidated his collection of pension plans and got his 'financial house' in order so he can plan for an early semi-retirement.

**Autumn**

With your career, family, home and savings in reasonable shape, your children will now be leaving home and you may find yourself able to have some fun for a few years before you start to wind down your career.

In this chapter I teach you about:

- ***Autumn is for harvest***
- Why you should reap and sow
- The importance of gaining clarity
- How it's time to smell the roses
- Wills, Trusts, Life Insurance and Lasting Power of Attorney
- How Stephen managed to work less, play harder and still have enough to retire.
- How Sue managed to leave her exhausting job much sooner than expected.

**Winter**

Now retirement or semi-retirement are in effect and you start to think about what you should be doing with your hard-earned money, how to safeguard it for the future while leaving lasting legacies that may be both financial and philanthropic.

In this chapter I teach you about:

- ***Winter is for 'putting your financial garden to bed'***
- Making the most of your resources
- Being prepared for health and care costs
- Protecting and passing on your pension and income
- How to set up a foundation
- Wills and Trusts in Winter
- Estate planning
- Passing on your non-financial legacy
- How retired Jim saved £1 million on the inheritance tax his children would have to pay, left a £2 million legacy to his grandchildren and lived the dreams that he had buried. He also made sure that his wealth could 'cascade' through his direct descendants (his bloodline).
- Meet Uncle Chacha-ji who refused to listen to advice and frittered away the family estate.

**The Four Seasons Matrix**
Here's the chart you need to copy and pin on the wall!

**Time to Write**
This is the place for you to make a note of your finances: write down a list of what you own and where it is kept to simplify your financial records for those you leave behind.

## PART TWO - BEYOND WEALTH

### True Wealth

Discover what being truly wealthy really means to so many people. You will find that, in the end, it's not just about money.

### Success to Significance

Come with me as I encourage you to find meaning, fulfilment and purpose in your life. Learn how to identify your *why*, *what* and *how* and move on to see how your legacy to the world can be richly rewarding.

### In the End

A quick overview in which I explain why there is no point in chasing the crock of gold at the end of the rainbow.

**"Bury my body and don't build any monument. Keep my hands out so the people know the one who won the world had nothing in hand when he died."**

*Alexander the Great*

# INTRODUCTION

We leave this earth as we arrive – with nothing.

We work, we play, we create, we reflect and we reap what we sow.

This book is a philosophical glimpse into the powerful insights and lessons that nature can give us about our lives and our relationship with wealth.

Life and wealth are like the changing seasons; inextricably linked. Just as the Seasons of your Life change, so must your Seasons of Wealth.

There are four things you can do with your wealth. You can spend it, save it, invest it or give it away. In nature too, you can choose to nurture it, harvest it, store it or do all you can to replant it for the following Spring.

The Seasons of Nature, though complex, are beautiful to witness and they, like us, move from one inevitable phase to the next. Nothing stands still. Each season prepares for the one to come.

Spring signals new life, freshness and birth. The gardens, fields and lanes are ablaze with colour. Life feels good, filled with promise. We bask in every opportunity to enjoy the sunny days.

Then there is the Summer. Shrubs and flowers flaunt their finery. The air is filled with the buzzing of bees. The days are long and warm.

Next comes Autumn with its tapestry of scarlet reds, rustic browns, golden yellows and sunset oranges. Harvests are rich. Creatures fatten up and store for what's ahead. There's a chill in the air.

Finally, there's Winter. Days shorten. Nights descend quickly. Frost nips your nose, ears and toes. Outside it's crisp and biting, or grey and sodden, chilling your bones when the wind picks up. Snowy, blue-sky days, emerald with holly are brightened by scurrying robins, ensuring this season is not all doom and gloom.

The Seasons become part of the rhythm of our souls.

It doesn't take a great deal of imagination to recognise that the four Seasons mirror our own Lives. If you understand this then you will always see there are four Seasons of Wealth.

It is of paramount importance that we recognise the connection between the Seasons of our Life and Seasons of our Wealth. Or, as the years go on and our lives move from Summer to Autumn and then finally to Winter, we will become increasingly confused about the best things to do with our wealth.

Just as the Autumn leaves fall, the Autumn Season of Wealth does not last forever. We need to manage our wealth accordingly and not leave it too late.

If you wish to have harmony in your life you need to make the appropriate changes to align happiness in your life with financial happiness.

JOIN ME UNDER THE MAPLE TREE

Let me ask you a few Tough Love Questions designed to get you thinking about your own financial life:

1. What Season of Life are you in right now?

2. What Season is your Wealth in right now?

3. Is there a mismatch between your Season of Life and Season of Wealth?

4. If so, what changes would you like to make?

5. What action are you now going to take?

6. Who can you share details of your actions with so you are accountable?

# PART ONE

# THE SEASONS OF WEALTH

*"Just as nature's seasons transition so beautifully from one to another, so should your life and your wealth. When we take action with that recognition, we reap the rewards. Not just in financial wellbeing.*

*We can use each season to improve the richness, enjoyment, fulfilment and the meaning of our lives."*

*Parminder Bains*

# IN THE BEGINNING...

My family originates from a small village called Moela Wahidpur in the Garden of the Punjab; the land of the five rivers and one of the most fertile lands on the planet. My ancestors were farmers for many generations. Home to them was a small house and a number of farm sheds on a small patch of land. Life was basic but happy.

Moela Wahidpur is in the district of Hoshiarpur, North India, and around 800 kilometres from the Himalayas in Nepal. Garshankar, the nearest market town, is about three kilometres away.

Mango trees grow abundantly in our region where the main crops are wheat, rice, sugarcane, maize, barley, other fruit and vegetables. My family lives off the land and milks the buffaloes.

In theory, Moela Wahidpur experiences four seasons although no one has ever seen snow. Winter and Spring take place from October to March bringing a chill to the air and misty mornings. A scorching Summer follows and then an Autumnal rainy or monsoon season.

With a hand to mouth existence, entirely dependent on the kindness or otherwise of the seasons, poverty caused my father and mother to emigrate to the UK in search of a better future. They had responded to an advert in a local Punjabi paper about the need for factory workers.

They arrived in Wolverhampton with just two pounds.

Life was hard. Neither spoke any English and they experienced a lot of racism. They laboured in the factories, worked long hours and lived from pay cheque to pay cheque for many years struggling to save money. The little money they managed to save was sent back to India to help their families.

My parents were very loyal to their roots and grateful for the chance to escape abject poverty.

## In Search of My Money Crop

I could see how hard life was for my parents and as a teenager I took on a series of casual jobs to help out. In my first ever part-time job as a 14-year-old, I sold Avon door to door at evenings and weekends. You may have heard of the Avon Lady. Well, I was the Avon Man. It was so much fun at 14 to meet all those prospective purchasers! I became quite good at it.

Next, I started a weekend job selling double glazing door to door on a commission only basis. I worked in the first drive-through McDonald's in Wolverhampton when I was 16 and helped out in an Indian takeaway. I also spent a couple of years helping a family friend shoot wedding videos at weekends. All this while I was still at secondary school and all the money I made I gave to my parents.

I became very good with numbers and became the

first of my ancestors to graduate from university – with an Honours degree in Accounting and Finance.

From early on I could see how important it was to save into three pots:

1. Short term
2. Medium term
3. Long term.

I understood the importance of having a budget, making tough choices and sticking to them.

It wasn't easy. I didn't always stick to budget but took small steps every day to form good money habits, always thinking of my parents and the brave and pioneering steps they took to find their money crop.

Over time, I grew to realise that there was more to life than money and that it was shallow to measure success through money and possessions.

## Gifts and Talents

My parents' first gift to me was to help me see that life had meaning beyond money and purpose beyond possessions. Not only have they shown this to me through their courageous actions to come to a new country, they have done it through their faith.

Culture and tradition are important to us. Gratitude and faith run as a thread through Sikhism and many life lessons are passed down through the generations.

The three key strands are *Kirat Karo* which means 'earn an honest living', *Vand ke shako* which means 'share with others' and *Naam Japo* which means 'keeping God in mind at all times'.

The second gift my parents gave me was their unwavering belief in the power I have to share my knowledge and talents to serve some and to bless others.

Today, as a Chartered Financial Planner, I am technically qualified to help people with their, often complex, financial situations. But what I have come to understand is that money only has meaning when it is put to good use.

The biggest service I can provide is to use my knowledge, gifts, talents and technical ability to help people create the kind of lives they really want and to help them live out their dreams.

## Nature's Reminder

Life is fragile. Fast forward to May Bank Holiday 2004. Early Summer and Mother Nature was starting to bring forth the fruits of her Spring labour. My wife, Satbir, and I were expecting our first child.

I remember the cherry trees in our back garden in full bloom and insects buzzing around. The air smelt fresh and our first baby was due anytime.

Satbir and I were feeling excited and a bit nervous at the same time. Life was rich and sweet. Aman was born on the Friday and weighed just over 5lbs. Like any new father, holding our new baby for the first time filled me with tremendous joy and slight trepidation as I wondered about the responsibility that came with this brand new, precious life in my hands.

It wasn't long before we realised that Aman was poorly – in fact she was very poorly. As my wife and I sat and waited for the consultant, we looked over the crowded car park towards the new family-sized car we had bought in exchange for our new, bright red, top-of-the-range Mercedes coupé.

The sun beat down outside but Satbir and I felt cold with fear. We were soon to discover that our baby daughter's blood was being pumped the wrong way around her heart. Our tiny, defenceless Aman was too small to be operated on and so we were told to take her home and that death was a real possibility within a couple of months.

We were given a white 'Doctor on Call' sign for the car, allowing us to park where we liked and visit whenever we needed. We knew this was serious. Satbir and I felt completely and utterly helpless and, for us, being parents became meaningless. All we had was hope and prayer and we leaned heavily on our faith. There was no instant cure. For five whole months we pushed through the tests, three hospital visits a week and the waiting, waiting, waiting. Each week a counsellor would visit us at home to discuss the reality of our situation. We just went through the motions of life.

At five months, Aman was big enough for the operation she needed. A cure was possible! It was a miracle. It was unimaginable to be a father and yet impotent, unable to go to the rescue of somebody you love beyond all imagination. Useless in heart, mind and action.

## Life's Reminder

As if nearly losing a child wasn't enough.

Two weeks before the operation, my boss called me into his office and told me to sit down. The City firm I was working for was under new ownership and they were making significant redundancies.

"Parminder, I am afraid we have to let you go," he said before looking away, out the window, so as to distance himself from my anguish at what was already an agonising time.

"My daughter is having her operation in a few days. I know where my loyalties lie," I replied. I was both furious at the injustice of the timing and rather pleased I could now go home to Satbir and Aman, where we knew exactly what mattered most – and it wasn't spending more time in the office.

"I'll clear my desk now," I finished.

At that moment I knew I had a bigger cause to answer to.

Luckily, the operation was a success.

So, there I was, thinking I was well qualified and could solve financial problems. That I could go and get anything I wanted. But this time my education, skills and money counted for nothing.

The whole experience was a vast learning curve. I was not in control.

There are certain principles in life that control us and over which we have no power.

I was not in control and neither are you.

We can't control the Seasons of Nature or Seasons of Life, but we can control the Seasons of Wealth. There is much to be gained from realising this truth.

When we recognise this truth and take action, that realisation allows us to reap the rewards, not just in financial wellbeing.

We can use each season to improve the richness, the enjoyment, fulfilment and meaning of our lives. But we tend only to do that when we work with the time-tested principles and collective wisdom of wealth.

Recognising the connection between the Season of our Life and the Season of our Wealth is a fundamental step on the path towards financial happiness and life's richness.

When we see these connections, we think differently. When our thinking changes, our financial behaviour becomes more effective. When our behaviour transforms, so too does the quality of our life.

JOIN ME UNDER THE MAPLE TREE

1. What does your family tree look like?

2. How did your parents start the search for their money crop?

3. How did you start your search for your money crop?

4. If I asked you how you would bring more meaning to your wealth, what thoughts would that question conjure up?

5. So, what's stopping you?

6. What's your next step?

*"In Spring we start our journey new,*
*When flowers bloom and skies are blue;*
*The trees are budding, birds will sing,*
*With youth in bloom it's always Spring."*

*Joseph Anderson*

# SPRING

## Nature's Spring

Spring is associated with new beginnings; leaves and plants start to grow and many flowers bloom. Temperatures increase and the days get longer. Farmers are busy ensuring every crop can reach its maximum potential.

## Life's Spring

In the Spring of our lives we are bursting and shooting up and blossoming. We're learning and educating and fighting to find out what the world is all about and how we can change it. We're the stalk that shoots from the seed.

We feel excited about the future. We are full of optimism and gain a great sense of enjoyment when we try new things. We have little life experience but we have become responsible for our own decisions, successes and failures. We start to earn our own money and make wish lists for what we can spend it on.

We recognise we are not too sure about what we are doing, we grope around during these early years and understand it's a time for learning, for discovering ourselves and seeking out new opportunities. We get to experience dynamic thinking and bursts of new energy. We meet new people, enter into new relationships and develop networks of social and professional contacts. It's certainly a time for fun.

Of course there are a few false starts and some thunderous mistakes along the way. Slowly, we start to realise that negative experiences are not all bad. They are the fertilisers that can serve us well and impact our future growth. Ultimately, we are grateful for these opportunities to learn.

**"There are no mistakes in life, only lessons."**

*Robin S Sharma*

These lessons, when learned well, will in turn serve us well, providing clarity and confidence for the future. Humans, like plants, must continue to grow if they are to thrive.

**"If you are green you're growing, if not you rot."**

*Parminder Bains to his children, more regularly than they appreciate!*

## Wealth's Spring

Now is the time:

- We get our careers off the ground.
- We begin to feel happiness associated with a steady income.
- We try to create a discipline of saving for the future.
- For nesting.
- To build an emergency pot.

It's important that at this stage in our lives we are clear about what we want and need in the short and longer term. Most people in life do not *plan to fail, they fail to plan.* If you don't know where you are going you may never get there. Whether entering a new relationship, having a child or getting a new puppy, we benefit from having a plan in place first.

## Financial Planning

In the Spring of our lives it's important to establish good money habits. The key is to create a healthy money habit of saving money right from the first pay cheque and then keep on doing so. Every time your income goes up, save some more. Remember to think in terms of giving yourself a permanent pay cut.

It is also a good idea to start an emergency fund. A good rule of thumb is to end up with six months' salary saved. It may also be time to think of mortgages and the protection of any debts should you fall ill, have a serious illness or even die prematurely.

Another of my favourite mantras, one I tell my children so regularly they have begun to roll their eyes when I say it, is:

**"Easy choices, hard life.**
**Hard choices, easy life."**

*Jerzy Gregorek*

### *Spend, save, give*

I have taught my children, who are in the Spring of their own lives, to save their pocket money into three pots:

- Save
- Spend
- Charity

The sooner we all get into good money habits the better.

### *A rainy day with the Bains family*

I remember one particular rainy day so clearly. The children were all at home and complaining of being bored so I suggested they come and help me tidy my study. That idea was met with resounding enthusiasm as I am sure you can imagine! Tidying up isn't much fun at any age but is even worse when you are aged four, eight or fourteen. We all crammed into my home office overlooking our leafy garden with that soaring maple tree and I soon set them to work with the paper shredder.

"Dad, are you going pay us?" asked Amrit, eight, looking up from the shredder.

Immediately, I realised that this was the perfect day for a lesson in finance. "Well, kids, what do think money is actually for?" I asked as I watched three foreheads crease in thought.

"Buying things?" suggested Karam, four, who was at the age when he was only interested in what he could have or get.

"Yes, Karam. What else?"

"For holidays?" added Aman, 14, who already seemed to love travel.

"Yes, and?" I continued, enjoying making them think.

"Is there something else, then?" Amrit asked. She looked confused.

"What about when we went to India and your mother gave you some money to give to the blind children?" I asked.

"Oh yes! So you can give it to other people, I suppose," she replied thoughtfully. All three of my kids have a caring streak.

"Yes! And how did that make you feel?"

"Sad because the children were blind and cold and poor and no one loved them."

"What would happen if people didn't give them money, then?" I asked, determined to make them think.

"No one would help them?" Aman said.

"So that's what charity's for, Dad, is it? Using money to help other people who aren't as lucky as us." Amrit paused and looked at me cheekily. "So are you going to pay us then, Dad? Or are we doing it for charity?"

"I will pay you something, you cheeky monkeys, but I want you to start putting the money you are given into three pots. One for saving, one for spending and one for giving away."

Today, a year later, saving and giving are natural to them. They still ask to get paid though.

## Saving

### *Planting the right money seeds*

All creation starts somewhere and in nature it always starts with a seed. The most fascinating seed I know of is the bamboo. In particular, the giant timber bamboo.

You may be astonished to know that the giant timber bamboo seed, once planted, shows no evidence of growth in its first, second and third years. It is just watered again and again and again by the farmer. However, in the fourth year it shoots up by 90 feet in 60 days.

How tall will it grow? As tall as it wants to. That's amazing.

During the first three years everything is happening under the soil. The giant timber bamboo builds a very deep root system to support its growth.

What is of particular value is that it teaches the farmer patience, courage and persistence. It teaches him about belief and self-discipline.

### *Growth*

The seed should grow, flower and, in turn, create a crop of new seeds. Nature shows us clearly that there are no limits to what we can harvest.

The giant timber bamboo needs patience and discipline as it is nurtured by a farmer who trusts in the process. His trust comes from past experience and knowing other farmers.

Belief and self-discipline are two crucial skills needed when starting to plant the seeds that will form the roots of your money crop.

### *How to tend to your money crop*

If you want to have an easy life in later years then the key is to develop sustainable money habits. Getting comfortable with getting uncomfortable will not only grow your financial resource it will also help you grow as a person.

Having spent over 10,000 hours interviewing successful people, the major difference between successful and unsuccessful people is that successful people have built up a habit of doing the things that unsuccessful people know they need to do but don't.

It is much easier to spend all your income each month rather than settle with the hard choice of saving, say 10%, as soon as it comes in. Try setting up an automated direct debit or standing order that goes directly into an investment plan with potential to grow. That done, you're free to go ahead and spend the rest of your income.

### *When is the best time to plant a tree?*

The wise answer is 50 years ago, so that you can sit in the shade of its branches now. Hindsight is a wonderful thing. The earlier you can start saving the better. Like a seed, the best thing you can do with your money is to help it grow. One of the easiest ways to do this is called compound interest.

**"Compound interest is the eighth wonder of the world. He who understands it, earns it. He who doesn't, pays it."**

*Albert Einstein*

This is a very simple principle and for anyone who wants to build lasting wealth, understanding and harnessing the power of compound interest is essential. **Compound interest is simply the interest that you earn on your interest.**

Let me show you how it works.

The following figures are based on an individual who:

- Earns £30k per annum
- Invests 10% of his salary, i.e. £3k per annum, or £250 per month
- Invests from age 20 to 60, i.e. over a period of 40 years

We assume inflation of 2.5% per annum and a rate of return of 5% per annum.

| At age | Fund based on £250 per month | Fund based on £300 per month (i.e. including 20% tax relief) | Monetary difference tax relief makes to fund growth |
|---|---|---|---|
| 30 | £43,256 | £51,907 | £8,651 |
| 40 | £126,689 | £152,027 | £25,338 |
| 50 | £279,752 | £335,701 | £55,949 |
| 60 | £551,954 | £662,344 | £110,390 |

### *The second best time to plant a tree?*

Today.

You need patience. It takes time.

Well, you can't hurry a tree, can you?

## Meet the Client

### *Meet John*

John had recently graduated and started a new life with a top firm of accountants in the City. The problem he brought to me was that he wanted to stop renting with his university friends and buy a house but did not know how much to save and where.

It soon became apparent that the real problem was that his friends were still 'financial teenagers' while John wanted to grow up. He painted me a picture of what he wanted his financial landscape to look like 30 years from now and we worked out that it was entirely possible.

**So... what did we do?**

John agreed to save 10% of his income and half his future bonuses 'come what may' towards his financial plan so that he could achieve financial happiness. We also built in some flexibility so that he could treat himself every once in a while. We met on a regular basis to keep his plan on track and several years on he mentioned how awesome it was to realise what could happen from simple habits.

"I now know I can have my house paid off and retire 10 years before I get my state pension," he told me. "That freedom of choice is important and very rare in the City, where it is easy to get trapped. Your reassurance meant that I could do it."

"In the early days, I used to get a lot of stick from my mates," he continued, "but now they congratulate me and even look up to me as they cannot shake off the bad money habits they have. I certainly didn't expect that."

JOIN ME UNDER THE MAPLE TREE

1. What does your financial landscape look like?

2. Are your financial pots organised?

3. If not, what's stopping you?

4. What influences your relationship with money?

5. What attitudes to money might you have inherited from your parents or other family members?

6. If you do not make changes to your behaviours as regards to your finances, where might you be in five years' time?

7. Of all the people you know, who do you think handles their money in the most positive way and what can you learn from them?

8. What would change in your world if you inherited enough money to meet your financial needs for the rest of your life?

*"Gather ye rosebuds while ye may,*
*Old Time is still a-flying;*
*And this same flower that smiles today,*
*To-morrow will be dying."*

*Robert Herrick*

# SUMMER

## Nature's Summer

This is the engine of it all.

Summer is a time between sowing and reaping. It is associated with watering, weeding, blooming and flourishing.

In the Summer the farmers water and weed their fields. They labour with love as they joyfully inspect their fields daily, in anticipation of a rich harvest. The days are long and warm and our farmers can see that all the preparations and work done in the Spring are starting to pay off.

It is easy to treat this as a time for kicking back and relaxing, for basking in the warm sun and putting off any thoughts about the future.

**"No one thinks of Winter when the grass is green."**

*Rudyard Kipling*

This is no time to rest on our laurels and sit back and watch our gardens grow. We still need to keep weeding, feeding and nurturing our crops.

## Life's Summer

During the Summer Season of our Lives we usually find ourselves in a period of creating, developing our skills and talents, achieving goals and objectives and enjoying life to the fullest. We are feathering our nests and growing our families and careers. We work hard but hopefully have some fun and joy along the way as well.

Fun is important and balance vital. However, too little or too much can be dangerous.

You can kill a plant both by watering it too much or by not watering it at all. No amount of professional success is worth the expense of failure in your personal life in order to achieve it.

While your young family grows and thrives, you may find that work commitments increase considerably too, leaving you with little time for yourself or for making important decisions. It is a well-known fact that people pay more attention to planning their summer holiday than they do their retirement!

We soon realise that our children are growing up fast and that *time*, not *money*, has become our most valuable commodity. We have no time-machine or magic formula for cramming more hours into the day.

**"The person who chases two rabbits catches neither."**

*Confucius*

It is during Summer that we start to ask ourselves some big questions. They usually take place around late Summer, sometime around our early 40s. Mid-life can cause a paradigm shift for us.

It is often a time when we take a long hard look at ourselves and consider changing how we live our lives.

## Wealth's Summer

Now is the time:

- We grow and develop and create more money.
- We work hard and play hard, reaping what Summer has to offer.
- We start to create and fund future generations.
- We need to preserve some of Summer's abundance to make the coming seasons more enjoyable.
- We begin to know how we want to spend the rest of our lives and how much money is needed to support it.

***Take stock and get your financial house in order***

It is important that we use our time wisely now. Here in the Summer Season of Wealth, we are in the acquiring stage of our lives and we still need to pause and take stock. We need to check in with ourselves often to make sure that our financial landscape is healthy and that we have been planting enough of the right seeds in Spring, so we can harvest what we are going to need in the Autumn. We need to give those seeds time to grow and strengthen if they are to yield the right fruit in the right quantities. Obviously, if we discover we planted the wrong seeds during the Spring we will not feel satisfied and hopeful in the Summer Season of our Lives. We need to continue the discipline of saving on a regular basis that we had started in the Spring Season. Just because it is Summer is no reason to give our savings a break too. This is necessary if we want to harvest financial happiness. It will be much easier to save if doing so becomes an ingrained habit. Making regular savings makes us more confident, even when the financial storms that we cannot control take us by surprise. During the Spring and Summer Seasons of Lives, we hunters and gatherers must continually acquire and build our financial asset base.

### *This is no time to be complacent*

It is likely that our earnings have gone up a fair bit since we started working and we are happily watching our various nest eggs starting to grow. In truth, there is not much difference between the Spring and Summer Seasons of Wealth. Both are a time for developing, maintaining and nurturing savings habits. The only difference is our own maturity and the lessons we have learned along the way. The more mistakes we make, the more we learn and the wiser we become.

## Financial Planning

Now more than ever, there is more pressure on us to take personal responsibility for our own financial health, just as we must for our physical health. We can't put it off any longer. It's now or never. We must get this right.

From now on we have to be careful that we live within our means and do not over-stretch ourselves and form bad financial habits born out of complacency.

Our responsibilities have increased over the Summer. If our parents are alive they may be getting older and perhaps more dependent on us. They are likely to need more of our time and maybe more of our money too, particularly if they develop healthcare or housing needs that the government cannot fund.

### *You may need to make sacrifices*

Many of us discover we have even less time for ourselves. Great sacrifices in our time, energy and money may need to be made.

It is now rare to have a job for life. We are all more vulnerable than ever.

## Meet the Client

### *Meet Paul*

I remember sitting with Paul, 38. He was very disillusioned with the future of work. He had accumulated half a dozen pension plans from his previous jobs. This is now a common reality for people in the Summer Season of their Lives.

He could not make sense of the mountain of paperwork and could see no logical connection between the pile of policies and plans he had accumulated... nor what he wanted to do with his future. It was a meaningless mess.

When we had a meaningful conversation that went beyond figures and jargon, it became clear that the real reason he was so unhappy was that he felt like a fraud. He was working in the City and wanted to give off the impression to his wife and friends that he was good with money. Like many, he had neglected his own financial landscape.

The fact that he wasn't managing to hold on to a job for more than five years made him feel inadequate.

**So... what did we do?**

I suggested that we take a look to see whether he could save money on his expenses – both personal and on his pension. Of course he could! I have yet to come across a person that has not been able to save money somewhere.

We helped him transform his total confusion into clarity.

Even better – we saved him over £6,000 a year in mortgage interest and redirected this to his pension pot, without affecting his standard of living.

Paul now has a simple consolidated pot where everything is in one place and has also saved thousands of pounds in management fees every year.

He now has what he calls, "a proper financial plan to take me to semi-retirement."

"You have stopped me making financial mistakes and got me more organised," Paul said. "I don't need to worry anymore and know everything is going to be okay."

## What Are Your Freshest Thoughts?

JOIN ME UNDER THE MAPLE TREE

1. What is the financial abundance of your Summer?

2. List three things on which you could spend money that would give you the greatest satisfaction.

3. How sustainable are your financial arrangements in the event of unforeseen circumstances?

4. What, if anything, would have to change in your finances to make you feel totally safe and happy?

5. When will you know you have enough?

6. What are your financial blind spots?

*"I like the Spring, but it is too young. I like the Summer, but it is too proud. So I like best of all Autumn, because its leaves are a little yellow, its tones mellower, its colors richer, and it is all tinged a little of sorrow... its golden riches speak not of the innocence of Spring, nor of the power of Summer, but of the mellowness and kindly wisdom of approaching age. It knows the limitations of life and is content."*

*Lin Yutang*

# AUTUMN

## Nature's Autumn

The start of Autumn will show a selection of gold, red and brown colours as the flowers and trees change.

Autumn represents the time for reaping the harvest you have planted and tended over the Spring and Summer Seasons.

Just as in Nature, these cycles repeat year after year.

**"I trust in Nature for the stable laws of beauty and utility. Spring shall plant and Autumn garner to the end of time."**

*Robert Browning*

If we are blessed with an Indian Summer there will be some unexpected, glorious, sunny days during Autumn too.

In the Autumn, the farmer is rewarded for his hard work. He reaps what he has sown. This is harvest time.

Nature teaches him every year and he hones his craft as he learns from his successes as well as his failures. He improves as a farmer and grows as a person. He accepts the yield of his harvest as his responsibility. He receives what he deserves, accepts this with good grace and continues calmly through the seasons as they arise.

With no time to waste, once the harvest is stored safely, our farmer must now get back to work. It is time to prepare the soil once more; tilling the land, digging, and pruning in readiness for Winter. It may be a time for celebration, sharing and coming together as a community, also for horticultural shows and harvest festivals. It is a time for finding new ways of thinking and focusing on the things that give life meaning.

## Life's Autumn

Some call this the Golden Years. If we are clever, if we are wise, if we are shrewd, we can turn all the hard work and experiences of our Spring and Summer into something magnificent and long-lasting. We can harvest all the hard work, blood, sweat and tears.

If we plan carefully, everything – our wisdom, our experiences our family and our money – will start to flow back to us.

If we are lucky we may have a period where we are neither financially responsible for our children nor our parents.

When we are in the Autumn of our Lives we can rely on the wisdom that comes with age, learning and making mistakes.

Harvest is about receiving as well as recognising

that it is okay to ask for help. Crops would rot if they were left out in the fields. When others come together to help out, everyone jointly experiences the harvesting accomplishment. It is the Season for accepting the transition of time and that we are maturing. It is only the farmer who faithfully plants in the Spring who can reap the harvest they deserve.

## Wealth's Autumn

Now is the time:

- We can choose how we spend our money now we are no longer responsible for children and perhaps generate an income from our assets, including a pension.
- We can afford some adventures.

With Summer done, it's time to enjoy some freedom and rewards for all your hard work.

If you have been wise with pension arrangements or are lucky enough to be in a final salary scheme, you may be able to enjoy an excellent harvest for 40 years of consistent hard work.

Likewise, in terms of Seasons of Wealth, if we have a well-designed financial plan and planted the right seeds in the appropriate Season, then we can look forward to a bountiful harvest.

In my experience, the key to successfully transitioning from the Summer Season of Wealth to the Autumn Season of Wealth is to be exceptionally clear on the purpose of your financial assets.

Time needs to be invested here to make sure you ask yourselves the right questions and gain a clear perspective of where you are actually headed. What crops, come Autumn, do you want and need to harvest?

## Financial Planning

It is easy to make too many assumptions without even realising you are doing so:

- "My work and state pensions will give me enough money to retire."
- "I will retire at 60."
- "I know I will probably have enough."
- "I will inherit something."
- "I can always downsize."
- "I can get a part-time job."

These are assumptions because none of these ideas come with a cast-iron guarantee. For example, much of our hoped-for inheritance could get swallowed up by a large unexpected inheritance tax bill or care home expenses. Both of these could impact your parents if they are alive. Part-time jobs tend to offer lower salaries. Our Boomerang Kids may need to live at home, and so on.

Once you agree with me (and I am sure deep down you do), the key question is how much do you need for the rest of your life? By this, I don't mean how much *will* you need once you retire, but how much do you actually need *now* and how much will you need *later*? How much do you need in total?

I encourage my clients to not just save religiously but to spend as well and have some fun. If you spend your life waiting for financial storms you will never get to enjoy the sunshine.

**"As you walk down the fairway of life you must smell the roses, for you only get to play one round."**

*Ben Hogan*

This thinking process usually leads to a bucket list of dreams and aspirations, of things to do, experience and see.

A bucket list does not always need to cost money. Sometimes the best things in life are free.

A very common problem I see is the mismatch between the Seasons of Life in which you are living and the Season of Wealth your money is experiencing. It is of no surprise to see the impact of this situation severely affecting your life. The funny thing is, it is usually not until you stop and think, that you realise you are not actually putting what you want on your To-Do List. You're not making time for *you*. Time just to think and ponder. I mean to really think literally about what matters and to not just continue pedalling on the hamster wheel of life, which seems to get precariously faster every single year. This *busy-busy* routine becomes very addictive, especially in the City, where everyone we see is doing the same thing and pedalling faster and faster.

Being trapped in this cycle of simply acquiring and consuming only ends in tears. At the end of life, no one is going to wish that they had spent more time in the office.

You may feel like you don't have time for *this*. I would respectfully disagree. You can't afford *not* to. I have seen many clients undergo amazing transformations in their lives just by thinking very clearly when they are with me. Everything we do is based on the quality of the thinking we do beforehand.

## Time to Think

We need to start thinking about what we are going to think about. Giving ourselves time to think will give us time to live. Just ask anyone who has had an experience of being close to death.

It should not have to take a life-changing illness for you to suddenly decide to make a change. We should all find a way to bring meaning to money and life well before a storm hits us and knocks the wind out of our sails.

Once most people have worked their way through the majority of their bucket list, their thoughts usually start to focus on other matters. This usually occurs during the later Autumn Season of our Lives and on the cusp of entering the Winter Season of our Lives.

Sometimes all it takes to make a change is to have someone ask you the right questions and help you to see your financial landscape in a different light. As humans, we tend to get in our own way.

***"You can change: you're not a tree!"***

*Jim Rohn*

## Other Financial Tools

While you are busy in the Autumn of your life it is easy to put off thinking about some of the financial nitty gritty. However, this is just the time you should be thinking about some things that will put you in good stead in the future. One of the most important of these is to make sure you have a suitable Will.

Though some useful financial tools can be set up in the Winter of your life, it is never too early to think about them.

### *Wills*

Wills are essential.

A **Will** or testament is a legal document by which someone (the testator) expresses their wishes as to how their property is to be distributed at death, and names one or more persons (the executor(s)) to manage the estate until its final distribution.

It's important to make a Will, whether or not you consider you have many possessions or money, as if you die without a Will, there are rules which dictate how money, property and possessions are allocated and this may not be in the way in which you would wish them to be distributed. For example:

- Unmarried partners and partners not registered in a civil partnership cannot inherit from one another, unless assets are held jointly, in which case the survivor will inherit due to survivorship.
- If you have children, you'll need to make a Will so that arrangements for the children can be made if either one or both partners die. If both partners die with no Will then the courts can decide unless other provisions have been made.
- It may be potentially possible to reduce the amount of tax payable on larger estates if advice is taken in advance and certain Trusts are set up in the Will. The main benefit is you can reduce generational inheritance tax for the children.

- If your circumstances change, it's important to amend any pre-existing Will accordingly. For instance, if you've separated and your ex-partner now lives with someone else or enters into a registered civil partnership as the previous Will is still valid. A previous Will is only invalid if you remarry.

Throughout my professional working life another common error I've seen is that families know they need to make a Will but they never get round to it. Either they are too busy and it never makes it to the top of their To-Do List, or they bury their heads in the sand because they do not want to talk about the possibility of death.

We all need to have more grown-up conversations. Only two thirds of the UK population has a Will. It does not matter how great the financial plans are that my clients implement, without a suitable Will and some relevant Trust planning, these plans will behave inefficiently after they die.

Then there is divorce. The divorce rate for the over 60s (silver splitters) is increasing faster than for any other age group.

The people you leave behind can be left with a devastating problem that is painful from both a financial and emotional perspective. There are also practical considerations to consider that we don't even think about.

It is not sufficient to have a Will written up by a solicitor who will just take your instructions. You need to involve someone who understands the way the Will interacts with inheritance tax, particularly if you have a large estate or children from a previous marriage.

I ensure that my clients' Wills are reviewed when they start working with me and, if they are not suitable for their needs, I ensure they are amended or replaced with an appropriate estate distribution plan.

With the right Will personal and financial affairs are optimised in the event of a death. Assets are passed to the right people at the time. The wrong people include HMRC and The Treasury, not just the son who is not good with money or the daughter-in-law from hell.

Losing a close family member is painful enough. Surely you don't want to cause more emotional and financial problems? A Will, combined with bespoke financial planning in place, will save unnecessary tax and lift the lives of your descendants and any charitable organisations you support.

By the way, it is perfectly legal to mitigate inheritance tax in ways that HMRC approves.

### *Lasting Power of Attorney*

A lasting power of attorney (LPA) is a form of power of attorney that allows the donor to appoint someone they trust to make decisions on their behalf once they no longer wish to or if they lose capacity.

Someone can lack mental capacity if they have an injury, disorder or condition that affects the way their mind works. This could mean they have difficulty making decisions all of the time or that it might take them a long time to make one.

### *Two forms of LPA*

An LPA can take one of two forms that are distinct and separate from one another and are completed using separate forms. They are:

1. Health and Welfare LPA (also known as a health and decisions LPA). This gives the attorney power to make decisions about the donor's healthcare and personal welfare.

2. Property and Financial Affairs LPA (also known as a financial decisions LPA). This gives the attorney power to make decisions about the donor's property and financial affairs.

Anyone aged 18 or over with the capacity to do so can make an LPA appointing one or more attorneys to make decisions on their behalf. It is not possible to make an LPA jointly with another person. Each person must make their own.

A recent survey carried out by the Office of the

Public Guardian found that 75% of people think that their partners or close family members can automatically make decisions for them if they're unable. As next of kin, many people expect that making medical decisions or future planning for loved ones is straightforward. This is NOT true; only an LPA gives a person the legal ability to give those they trust the power to make decisions on their behalf if they were to lose mental capacity.

LPA registrations in the UK more than tripled between 2010 and 2015 from 129,000 to 441,000. With mental health continually in the headlines, this figure has now comfortably surpassed the 2 million mark.

In January last year, my 65-year-old mother-in-law unfortunately contracted double pneumonia here in the UK. She was extremely ill and it was an emotionally-testing time for everyone. The NHS were brilliant and she received the highest standard of care I have ever seen. In the end she was sedated for around eight months while they gave her treatment and she survived a terrible ordeal. She is now returning back to normality slowly. It was touch and go for a while and we realised we needed to have had an LPA for health and welfare in place in case we had been required to make a decision for her at a time when she was clearly unable to. Just having a Will is not enough.

This experience made our family stop and think about what, if any, decisions we may have made differently. We soon made sure that everyone in the family had reviewed their Wills and had the necessary Lasting Power of Attorney(s) in place.

"I don't want my children left in the dark and not knowing what to do if this happens to us," Satbir said soon afterwards. "Even though there is a cultural gap between my parents and me and we have different expectations about who will look after whom in the event of ill-health or old age, I want to make sure I make my own instructions very clear."

Don't wait for a storm to hit you. Be prepared in advance.

### *Trusts*

In the UK one of the most developed ways of maintaining control of your wealth and choosing what happens to it, particularly in the Winter of Life, is the use of Trusts.

Trusts are legitimate tools used by the wealthy to ensure money does not disappear out of the family. They are simple, non-contentious and effective.

They make sure that the money goes to the right person at the right time.

When someone (the settlor) gives property to another person (the trustee) to hold for the benefit of a third person (the beneficiary) this is called a Trust. A Trust is a way of holding and protecting your assets for the future and consists of a deed, which is the set of rules for how the Trust should be operated, setting out who the beneficiaries are, who the trustees are and how the Trust will be administered. Trusts can hold assets, invest and borrow money, operate businesses and also pay tax.

If this sounds a bit complicated, then let me explain in more detail:

***1. Settlor***
This is the person who creates the Trust. It's a bit like the person who is the founder of a company.

***2. Trustees***
These are the people who are responsible for managing and maintaining the Trust. Using the company example, they are a bit like the Directors.

***3. Beneficiaries***
These are the people who will benefit from the Trust in the form of capital or income. They are similar to shareholders in a company.

***4. Assets***
This is the wealth inside the Trust; a bit like the working capital you put into a company.

## *Life Insurance*

Life Insurance is a contract between an insurance policy holder and an insurer (or assurer), where the insurer promises to pay a designated beneficiary a sum of money (the benefit). The sum is paid out upon the death of an insured person (often the policy holder). Depending on the contract, other events such as terminal or critical illness can also trigger payment. Policy holders typically pay a premium, either regularly or as a lump sum. Funeral expenses can also be included in the benefits.

A Life Insurance policy can be used effectively to pay for a fund on your death in order to pay any inheritance tax bill. You can even get the beneficiaries of your estate to pay the premiums. Just make sure the plan is in the right type of Trust.

This is also an effective way of giving you permission to spend while you are alive, knowing your inheritance bill will be paid in this way when you are gone.

## Meet the Clients

### *Meet Sue*

Sue was 60 years old and living in Surrey when we met.

The problem she brought to me was the impact of her all-consuming job. By the time she reached home, at silly o'clock on a Friday evening, she felt utterly chewed up.

Drained of every ounce of energy... she couldn't even talk to her husband and children. Instead, she headed straight for her bedroom, accompanied only by a large G&T.

**So... what did we do?**

Together, we helped her transform abject misery into total financial happiness and freedom. We changed her investments from the growth phase to the harvesting phase and set that in motion right away. Within two months, Sue was confident enough to hand in her notice at work.

And we did that by showing her that she really *could* retire. She really could be free. And she could do that *today!*

Which is precisely what she did.

Was it all about money or something else?

Sue told me the real story behind the story and *why* she wanted to really retire early.

It was the reality of her real life situation that was key here.

Sue said what she really found meaningful was that, "I am no longer trapped in a hamster wheel. Your advice and skills have saved me from five years of complete misery. Most importantly, I can now spend quality time with my elderly mother, who only has a few years left."

***Meet Stephen***

Stephen, from Buckinghamshire, was in his early fifties. He was an executive by day and a cyclist on weekends. He loved nothing more than to escape into the country after a hard week in the office, taking to remote tracks and lanes with just his mountain bike for company.

He sat with me and told me that he was shot to pieces by stress and worry. He had been made redundant and was frenetically trying to find a new full-time role. The threat of unemployment and losing his professional status and recognition, not to mention his salary, terrified him.

However, he genuinely wanted to slow down and spend more time with his wife of 26 years, Julie, especially since the children had flown the nest.

The thing is... everyone told him he was too young to slow down and he was absolutely scared stiff.

**So... what did we do?**

I showed him that he actually had enough assets already and he could slow down the pace of his hectic life and spend quality time with Julie. He really could sleep well again.

So... we restructured his asset base and simplified his financial life. We also reduced the risk in his portfolio and preserved his assets.

"You are the only person who showed me that, actually, I have enough!" Stephen told me. "To keep my grey matter buzzing, I now have a part-time, less stressful role near where I live and am devoting more of my energy to quality time with Julie. We now have joy in our lives again. Thank you!"

JOIN ME UNDER THE MAPLE TREE

1. What will be the bounty of your harvest?

2. How much money do you need for the rest of your life?

3. How will you know when you have enough?

4. If you have more than enough, what are you going to do with the excess?

5. If you have less than enough, what are you willing to do to correct that?

6. What have you been financially tolerating that now needs attention?

*Winter's Bounty*

***"And now the harvest is completed.***
***The land is tilled,***
***the fruit is stacked in rows,***
***safe from the silvery voice of recession***
***whispering gently in the branches of***
***your day.***
***The sage is not afraid of hoarfrost.***
***Tomorrow's Spring will dawn anew."***

Parminder Bains

# WINTER

## Nature's Winter

During the Winter Season of Nature there is a kind of *shutting down*. Trees lose their leaves and suspend their growth, entering into a state of dormancy while they conserve their energy. Hibernating animals return to their dens.

Yet Nature never ceases to be interesting. There is still beauty. You can see the bright red berries on true winter flowering shrubs. There is a rainbow of colour in hedgerows, woodland, grassland and on the side of the road.

In Winter, the farmer stores and preserves the year's excess harvest so it can feed the family over the cold, unproductive Winter. This is a time for maintaining equipment, rest, recuperation and inward activity. The reduced daylight makes days shorter. Only the hardiest flowers can survive the harshness; farm scenery lacks its Spring and Summer colours.

Under the seasonal coverings of frost or snow, Nature appears to be sleeping, waiting for the warmer weather and longer daylight hours. This is an illusion. Nature never sleeps. There are subtle but vital changes taking place. Under the soil the cold temperature works its magic on the seeds, bulbs and roots. Without the cold of the Winter our gardens would be less beautiful in Summer. This colder temperature is essential to many plants. Some would neither grow nor flower without it.

Fruit trees use the nutrients and energy they store in Autumn to keep them going through the Winter. Bulbs need cold weather (ideally minus 10 degrees or colder) to stimulate stem growth. It is certainly evident that chilling weather plays an essential role in ensuring that the following Spring is as productive and beautiful as the last.

## Life's Winter

During the Seasons of Life, if we get our financial landscape right, we can transition from youth to middle age to a period of feeling fulfilled. One of the advantages of being older is that we will have gained wisdom during the preceding decades.

In the Winter Season of Life, our thoughts turn to making the most of our resources. After a lifetime of gain and acquisition, we now think about giving back. It feels wonderful to have the time and the means with which to replant, nurture and build on what has given us so much over the years. Maybe we take up voluntary work or non-executive positions. Maybe we start to mentor others following in our profession.

There is still time: time to think, time to do some of the things we have not yet done.

Now we need to concentrate time and energy on what's most important to us. Perhaps we will give back to the community and to the planet that has given us so much.

We think about how we want to be remembered and what our legacy might be, not only to our families but to the world.

This period of sitting back, taking stock and making the most of our bounty is an essential part of preparing for the next Spring, which is represented by our grandchildren. They are the future. We are now in a position to teach them about life and creating good money habits.

We have the time to play in the park with them and eat ice cream. We are not rushed. Life is simple – we do not have to go to work the next morning.

We are not going to hurry, we are just content. As I have said before: you can't hurry a tree.

During this Season of our Lives it is time to be still, to remember and reflect on what we have learned and what we have gathered. If we rush around too much, like we did in our working years, it could lead to restlessness, impatience and the inability to rest. It is against Nature.

Uncomplicating your life will do wonders for you. Every Season has a purpose and everything happens for a reason. Have you ever looked closely at the rings of a tree that has been chopped down? Besides trying to guess its age by counting the number of rings, there is a further powerful insight.

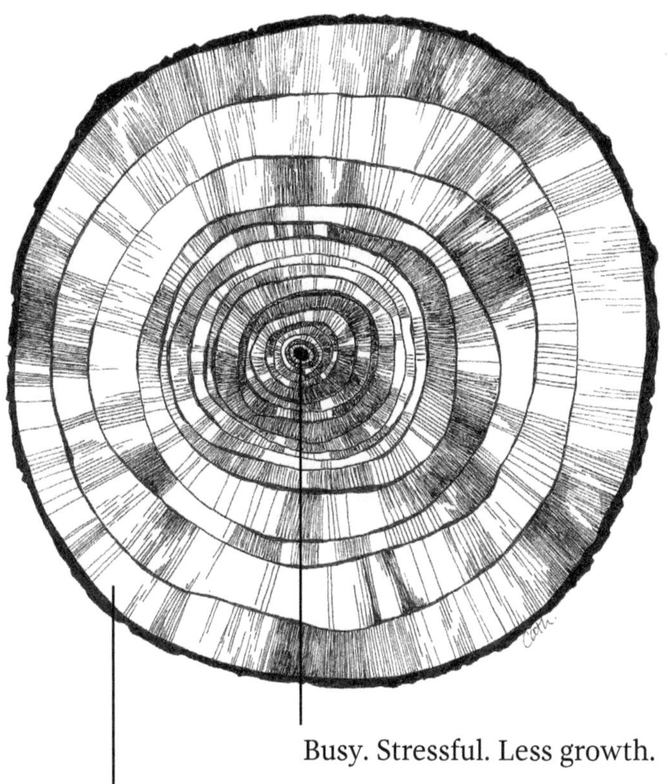


Some of the rings will be much closer together than the others and this is where there will have been less growth and perhaps some stress, a forest fire or disease maybe. Just like Mother Nature, the tree does the same. It slows right down and grows less than in the other Seasons. You too need to slow down and stop rushing around trying to get it right.

Admire each Season in its time.

If you plant a bulb when the ground is warm, it will become diseased and start to rot. Wait until it is Winter and freezing before you plant it. It is only in these conditions that it can do what it needs to, otherwise it will die. The soil in Winter is cold and frozen, bitter and sharp – an ideal environment for the bulb to gain strength and fight for the Spring to come. That is the beauty of Winter.

Just as the newly planted bulb draws its strength from the fallow earth, we too need to draw on our inner strength and start being a little more reserved and tactful. This is a time to be cautious and careful, to preserve our energy and not take on too much. Try to know your own limits as good caregivers and take extra care of your finances, possessions, car and home. Rest, relax and take time off to recuperate and recharge. Be grateful for your health and look after it. You only have one body to live in.

Winter coming after Autumn is part of the natural order of things. It cannot happen at any other time. We've learned our lessons.

Wisdom is knowledge put to good use.

**"In the midst of Winter, I found there was, within me, an invincible Summer."**

*Albert Camus*

In the midst of difficulties and hardships, Winter has an abundance of wisdom and patience. Patience means to endure, to be still. It means to wait and be quiet and not to hurry and rush.

**"The oak sleeps in the acorn, the bird waits in the egg."**

*James Allen*

You've probably heard the saying: "It is not the years left in your life, it's the life left in your years".

Look forward to tomorrow and the future with gladness and anticipation. Creativity is one of those things that keeps giving. Michelangelo did some of his best paintings past the age of 80. For Picasso, it was only once he was 90. Wright, the great architect, drew up his most amazing plans when he too was in his 90s. The scientist Edison was still inventing at a ripe old age and George Bernard Shaw wrote his great plays well into his senior years as well. The story continues with greats such as Galileo and Beethoven.

This serenity prayer is a perfect description of harmony in the Autumn and Winter Seasons of Lives:

**"God grant me the serenity to accept the things that I cannot change,**
**Courage to change the things I can**
**and the wisdom to know the difference."**

*Reinhold Niebuhr*

Trying to control things we cannot control drains our energy.

## Wealth's Winter

**Now is the time:**

- We may not be able to recycle our life but we can recycle our wealth.
- We can invest in the new Spring, younger lives.
- We ensure the next Spring fares well without us.

### *How to Protect Our Hard-Earned Harvest*

Having poured our hearts and souls, blood, sweat and tears into our life's work, the preservation of our hard-earned wealth, so that we have enough to be able to weather the Winter, is vitally important. Likewise, we want to ensure we can protect our estate in such a way that our descendants can benefit too, rather than giving it all to the tax-office. It is prudent to begin thinking about minimising any inheritance tax and to start to ensure that assets pass to the right people at the right time. Just as our farmer, too, needs to erect safe barns and warehouses for crops and find routes to market that will ensure these crops feed others while making a decent profit.

Most people want to be remembered after they leave this earth and thought needs to be given to leaving not just a financial legacy but also a non-financial legacy. The questions: "What should we do tomorrow?" or "What should we do next?" should be answered as you think about giving back.

**"Begin with the end in mind."**

*Stephen Covey*

As the wise sage you now are, in the Winter Season of your life, you are acutely aware that, like Nature, the Seasons of Wealth have their own rhythm. Economies do not simply keep on growing year on year. Just like Nature, they have their Seasons, they ebb and flow and ultimately collapse. This is part of the natural cycle of things. The end is inevitable. They then start growing again.

As we move from the late Autumn of our Lives to the Winter Season, we need to take precautions so that we don't get caught out. Learning from Nature is important. Storing and preserving what we have worked so hard to grow and harvest allows us to remain in control and gives us peace of mind and financial happiness. We worked hard to create our rich harvest. Where is the good in losing it right away?

Learning from Nature also allows us to evolve and build upon what we have gained and to improve on the seeds we will plant in the coming Spring; creating our legacy to the world. The wisdom that each Season of Wealth has given us can be retained so that we can plant and nurture more wisely the following Spring. This is our time to give back to the world that has been good to us.

## Financial Planning

Now that you have some time to take stock of your finances, let's have a look at some of the things you might want to use your nest egg for:

### 1. *Healthcare*

Recent studies show that residential care fees in the South East of England cost from £1,000 a week. Factor in that the average stay in a care home is about two and a half years and you're looking at a bill of about £52,000 a year, or over £130,000.

### 2. *Income*

Of course, you are also going to want a decent level of income for the rest of your own life and your spouse's life as well as any other financial dependants. You want your wealth to be preserved so that it keeps pace with inflation. This is often a key objective during the Winter Season of Wealth.

### 3. *Giving*

I have talked thus far more about spending, saving and investing your wealth than about the fourth option: giving it away.

**"The best way to hide your wealth is to give it away. If you are generous with your wealth, the money that would have disappeared sooner or later becomes an everlasting jewel, deeply engrained in the heart of the recipient."**

*Confucian scholar, Jeong Yak-Yong (1762-1836)*

If we are lucky enough to have excess wealth above what we truly need for the rest of our lives, deciding to help others is a natural objective. About 70% of the UK chooses to give to charity. We are the largest contributors in Europe and seventh in the world.

Many people want to contribute to society and have a growing desire to be seen doing good while taking advantage of the tax reliefs available. There may be a charitable cause that is close to your heart or that has touched your life. Luckily, the government incentivises us to gift our money this way, assuming certain rules are met. Gifts do not have to be financial – they can be physical assets too and you can give them during your lifetime and/or after your death. You can maintain some control over what recipients do with your money or relinquish control completely. Gifts can be made to institutions as well as to individuals.

Giving is a natural and normal act and helps build communities and promote shared values across generations. You can even involve children in the decision-making process, if it's appropriate. My clients tell me that doing so is rewarding and bonding. Using wealth wisely, for the greater good, brings meaning to people's lives. It's not uncommon to see my clients' philanthropic capital working as hard as their investment capital. Now there are also various charitable networks up and down the country where you can make donations that will have a direct impact on your own town or village.

No person is an island, and motivating society to give ever more effectively – helping to transform lives and communities around the globe – is natural, as is engaging and encouraging others to continue and extend our work once we are no longer here.

The government encourages you to give like this through incentives such as Gift Aid, which will reduce your tax bill. There is also a reduction in death duties payable when you give to charity.

Gift Aid is a tax incentive that enables tax-effective giving to charities in the UK. The charity receives an uplift in the amount they receive, currently set at 25%.

### *4. Setting up a Foundation*

A Foundation is a category of non-profit organisation or charitable Trust that typically provides funding and support for other charitable organisations through grants and that may also engage directly in charitable activities. Foundations can be public, such as community Foundations, or private, typically given, bequeathed or supported by an individual or family.

It's also possible to set up your own Family Foundation if this will excite you and you want even more control over how the money is spent. You no longer need to be a billionaire like Bill Gates in order to set one up.

Setting up a Foundation is not unrealistically complex either. You are also free to decide whether you want to change the objective and direction, close it when it has run its course, or leave it to run indefinitely as part of your future legacy.

## Your Will in Winter

We all like to think that the people we love will care for each other when we are dead. In reality there are no guarantees besides death and taxes.

When money is involved people's attitudes can and do change. The best time to make a Will is today. The best time to make sure your estate plan is in place is today. The Princess of Wales died at age 36 leaving an estate of £21.5 million. Yet, according to Worthy.com in February 2018 in an article called *Princess Diana's Will and Estate Revealed*, after inheritance tax of £8.5 million her net estate was just £13 million. She never did any inheritance tax planning!

## Your Trusts in Winter

A Trust makes sure that besides saving inheritance tax, the money goes to the right person at the right time. It ensures that it is not lost in a future divorce or bankruptcy case and protects against sideways disinheritance (inheritance passing sideways to a partner rather than down to natural children securing bloodline planning).

The best time to set up a Trust is today. Future legislation and regulation can change so it makes sense to set one up now to be used later.

Trusts can be set up during your lifetime, on death via your Will or both. Setting up a Trust during your lifetime could be rewarding as you would be able to see the benefits of your money while you are alive. You may also create a combination of both to ensure your hard-won wealth is used sensibly by the next generation and the next.

## Pensions and Inheritance Tax

Until recently, it was challenging to pass on pension funds through the family without incurring any inheritance tax. However, all of this changed on 6th April 2015 when new 'pensions freedom' rules came in.

Firstly, it is important to understand there is a difference on the tax treatment of how pension funds may be withdrawn, subject to the age of the member on death:

- Death of the pension fund member before age 75 allows for the inheriting individual to receive the pension fund as a pension fund in their own name without tax – they may also withdraw the entirety of this inherited fund without income tax, inheritance tax or capital gains taxes in their own name.
- On death occurring after age 75, the pension fund is passed to the receiving individual, again tax-free, but if they wish to withdraw it (as an income or a lump sum) they must pay income tax at their marginal rate.

In both scenarios, the pension fund can be inherited as a pension fund and no taxes incurred. Taxes may only potentially occur where a member dies after age 75 and the capital of the pension fund is already being withdrawn.

Naturally, under the new pension freedoms rule, an individual may choose when and when not to draw pension income. This is certainly not the case with all pension contracts; there are many different types and they may not all benefit from pension freedoms rules in their current format. This is a complex area and outside the scope of this book but can be discussed with a Chartered Financial Planner.

### *Perpetual inheritance*

Legislation permits one individual to pass their

pension fund to another and for the recipient to do so too. Accordingly, pension capital can cascade through a family tax-free on death (if not withdrawn from the pension wrapper) ad infinitum.

### *Estate planning*

The Winter Season of Wealth includes the acknowledgement that ultimately we MUST let go of our wealth.

That is not negotiable.

What is negotiable is *HOW* we let go.

How do we create that next Spring?

We call that creation process Estate Planning.

This is necessarily a time when your thinking goes beyond yourself. It's time for you to consider your loved ones, children, grandchildren, the community that nurtured you and those who were not as blessed as you.

Having helped hundreds of families, I have realised that clients wrestle with some common questions when they start to plan their estate.

### *The four common estate planning questions*

There are four main questions that clients often want to ask me when thinking about the future:

1. How do I make sure that my money ends up in the right hands at the right time?

2. How do I give my money to the next generation and still maintain control of that capital for me and still save inheritance tax?
3. How do I give my money to the next generation and still enjoy sufficient income to maintain my desired lifestyle and still save inheritance tax?
4. How do I do keep all of my wealth and yet not burden my children and grandchildren with the 40% inheritance tax bill when I die? See Jim's story later in this chapter.

### *Get a cash flow forecast*

The first thing you have to do though, is to make sure that you have enough wealth left for yourself and that you won't run out of money.

A well-prepared lifetime cash flow picture showing you the *shape* of your money will be really helpful here. Financial Planners like me work with sophisticated software that creates graphs out of the financial details you share with them. By simply changing a few figures or shifting priorities around you can see the impact of making various decisions and that includes doing nothing. For example, of moving from semi-retirement to full retirement over five years, downsizing or buying a holiday home. Maybe you want to know how much you should sell your business for and when, to allow you to do what you really want. Seeing this in full colour can be very helpful for clients, who start to understand what their money can and can't do.

Other scenarios may be, for example:

1. What happens if the stock market crashes by 25% – am I going to run out of money?
2. What would happen to my spouse if I died before/after them – are they going to be financially okay?
3. What would happen if I sell my house and rent instead – would it make a meaningful financial difference?
4. How much can I afford to give away and when?

Once you have done this you can now start to answer those *four common estate planning questions.* Often the solution is to use a suitable Trust arrangement. There are so many different types on offer that there is sure to be one to suit your needs.

## The Four Scariest Scenarios

Most of my clients worry about their money getting to the *right place at the right time.*

Are you also determined that your wealth will remain with your direct descendants? Do you want to be confident that it won't disappear out of the family in a few years?

You may not think this will happen to you but, believe me, the scenarios below can and do happen.

The four possible scary scenarios are:

1. You have the son or daughter-in-law from hell.
2. Your son or daughter is not good with money.
3. Your children eventually get divorced.
4. Your children become bankrupt.

In each of the above situations, money that you worked hard for leaves the family.

One thing that can prevent such financial disasters is what's called a Direct Descendant Trust.

## Three Things to Consider When Estate Planning

When considering how to plan an estate, it is necessary to address how the beneficiaries, most likely your children, will deal with the inheritance. You may want to safeguard against any unwise choices they may make.

It is important you do your best to mitigate any financial disasters and take problems such as bankruptcy, sideways disinheritance and illness into account.

Let's have a look at some of the most common problems here:

### *1. Long-term care*

If you have assets in excess of £23,250 you will have to pay for your own care home fees. This means you may have to sell your assets and this includes your family home.

Do you want your home and the money you wanted to pass on to your family to end up going to the Local Authority? Further, the Local Authority can, in theory, challenge any movement of capital if they believe that your sole motivation is to reduce your assets. Therefore, we do not encourage planning or activity that can be seen to have been carried out for this purpose.

If you own a family home your spouse may be forced to sell it on the occasion of your going into care to pay for fees.

What if you leave your estate to your wife and, after your death, she needs to meet long-term care costs, will the Local Authority take away any future inheritance for your children?

If you set up some Trusts as part of your overall estate planning and inheritance tax planning strategy well in advance of needing care from the Local Authority, then it is possible to ring fence assets from attack. Rules can and do change and it's best to forward plan when you are in good health.

### *2. Become Tenants in Common*

Another useful tip is to change the ownership of

your property to what is called Tenants in Common. In this way each person owns half the property. You then set up appropriate Wills and Trusts, each naming the other spouse as beneficiary, so that they can inherit the other half of the house upon the death of the other spouse. In this way the Local Authority cannot enforce the sale of half a house.

### *3. Remarriage*

What if your spouse remarries after you die and assets intended for your children end up leaving the family?

A recent study shows that 60% of men and 20% of women remarry or are in a new relationship within two years after the death of their previous spouse.

It really does make sense to think about reality here.

When there is a large age-gap between spouses it is fairly likely that the younger spouse will remarry should they divorce. While married they may have fully intended that the family home go to the couple's children, but after a divorce the home could move to the younger remarried partner's new family.

A Lifetime Trust can help here, stipulating that on the occasion of either of their deaths the surviving spouse owns half the house but has a lifetime interest in the other half.

***It pays to be prepared***

In short, my advice is very simple. Be practical and think ahead. The solution to all of the above is using the right Trusts and making changes to your Will. There are many different types of Trust so advice is essential. There is no need to worry.

## Making Financial Gifts

Most people understand that the earlier you plan the better and whilst the government provides plenty of exemptions on making gifts so that they are immediately out of your estate, they are still pretty small.

The most powerful one – sadly underused – is gifting out of your normal income. Again, there are rules to follow here but it is also possible to use Protective Trusts to protect the money that is being gifted to protect it from the four scenarios just mentioned.

Once a gift has been made, you normally need to wait a full seven years before it is considered outside of your estate for tax reasons.

***What if you cannot wait seven years?***

There are a number of other solutions available that take into account something called Business Property Relief and that are beneficial after just two years. Business Property Relief enables family firms to pass down through the generations. You can invest into companies that benefit from this. Again, further discussion is outside the scope of this book.

In addition, it is possible to transfer an ISA to another ISA that benefits from this two-year rule.

## Your Non-Financial Legacy

Many clients tell me that it is not just passing on their financial assets that matters most. It is important that they pass on a non-financial legacy too. Things like traditions, heritage, culture, money habits and life experiences they have learned from previous generations should not be forgotten. They care about their personal ethics, values and wisdom. Some want their journals and photographs, their paintings and artefacts to be passed on too. Nevertheless, talking about money can be difficult and we know that, especially in the UK, it's a thorny issue, almost a taboo subject. When I used to ask clients why they had not taught their children or grandchildren about money, they would typically say they never got around to it. In truth, they had just kept putting it off.

Money does not have to be an uncomfortable conversation. You don't need to wait until a significant milestone birthday. You cannot predict how long you will live. Nor can you predict how long a plant or tree will survive. Sadly, we all know we can't recycle ourselves and bloom again the following Spring. But we can recycle our wealth for many Springs to come through our children and grandchildren.

It's not so easy to ensure your tangible assets can survive the storms of time and continue to benefit future generations. It can be just as hard to ensure your intangible assets, such as your wisdom or ability to make a difference, will live on too.

### *Start the conversation*

If you are to have a hope of passing on your tangible and intangible legacies it is crucial that you nurture a strong culture of communication and trust while you are alive. You must develop a succession plan. This isn't just necessary for the high-flying business owner or entrepreneur who has sold their business for a fortune. You should sit down and prepare your children and grandchildren to take things over one day. For this to be effective, you should hold not one but regular meetings with your family.

If I ask young adults what they will do with money they inherit, their top two answers are usually to take a holiday and buy a sports car. You see, most of the time young adults are a bit like my son, Karam, earlier in this book who at four was only interested in what money would get him. Unless you have a serious conversation with them you can't expect them to think about money in a sensible and mature way.

There is a lot of evidence, especially in the US, that shows that much inherited wealth is depleted by the third generation. Many stories show families going from rags to riches and back to rags again within 100 years or so. The Vanderbilt family went from one of the richest to the poorest in three generations.

***"Give your children enough money that they can do something but not too much that they don't do anything."***

*Warren Buffet*

The purpose of this deep and meaningful family conversation is to build a common vision of what it is you actually want the money to do and, whilst everyone might have different views, I find that once you have satisfied money for living expenses or any desired dreams, philanthropy is usually the most sensible course of action. Such a conversation can bond families. Wealth can impact a family psychologically and unless it is handled carefully it can tear them apart as well as bring them together.

Psychotherapist Jessie O'Neill defines this problem as 'affluenza' in a book called *The Golden Ghetto*. She had inherited significant wealth herself and she went on to interview many others in the Forbes Rich List who had also inherited a large sum of money and she defines 'affluenza' as a dysfunctional relationship with money and the pursuit of it.

### *It depends on who you are*

The amount you save, spend, invest and give all depends on who you are and what you want.

We are all different and one size does not fit all. Gaining complete clarity on the purpose of your wealth is important. It is never too soon to create a vision for your wealth.

It really does not matter which cause you support, but most people end up choosing one aligned to their values, beliefs, struggles and life experiences that works towards the greater good. Life is given meaning when we use our gifts, talents and wealth to help and serve others. Do this and it will excite your passions and define a sense of purpose in your life. Yes, even in the Winter Season of Wealth!

See, I told you there was still plenty of beauty around in Winter!

### *Why does it matter that we leave a legacy?*

We all have our own views regarding the legacies we hope to leave. We are neither the Rain Forest Pirahã tribe that has no language for anything past or future, nor are we like the Ojibwe and Chippewa people who consider the impact on the next seven generations when they make a decision. Most of us are somewhere in the middle.

Leaving a legacy matters because, as humans, we care.

We cannot live forever, but if we are wise with our money, we may be able to create something that can.

## Meet the Client

### *Meet Jim*

Jim, a retired City fund manager, lived in Hampshire near the beach. His wife was Spanish and they had a home there that they loved to visit every month or so. He was passionate about sailing and was lucky enough to have a boat in both countries. They had a large family with three adult children and seven grandchildren whom he adored.

Jim had four huge problems. At least, he considered them to be huge:

1. He faced leaving an inheritance tax bill of around £1 million on his own estate.
2. He wanted to leave a legacy to his grandchildren after his death.
3. He wanted some extra income.
4. His father had passed away, leaving him with a £400,000 inheritance tax bill that he had to pay.

Jim was in a constant tug-of-war with himself and at a loss what to do.

**So... what did we do?**

By simply making a few changes we were able to achieve the following amazing outcomes:

1. We saved him that tax bill of £1 million that he would have left his children.
2. We created a legacy of £2 million tax free on his death.
3. We worked out how he could spend an extra £2,000 a week and never run out of money.
4. He found the money to pay his father's inheritance tax bill.

As Jim wanted to keep matters simple and still enjoy his money whilst he was alive, while looking after his descendants, we set up a life insurance policy in his name that would pay out £3 million into a Trust when he died.

This £3 million would be used to pay the projected £1 million inheritance tax bill and the balance of £2 million as a legacy to his children and grandchildren.

Together, in the late Autumn Season of Jim's Wealth, we created a tax saving and a remarkable financial legacy. Jim had achieved the happy ending he wanted.

Now Jim tells me that he knows how it feels to experience Nirvana in his *life*. Yes, you read that correctly. He knew that reaching Nirvana was not about *money*, but about his *life*.

What exactly does Jim mean, then? Every story has a Nirvana – a beautiful feeling of happiness and peace where life is sweet and rich.

Let's begin by looking at the facts.

**Is it about tax? Or is it about something else?**

"My father's tax bill put me firmly in the *doo dah*," he told me. "He landed me with a massive tax bill close to £400,000. I never ever want to burden my own children or grandchildren with such an emotional and financial mess. I want them to see the benefit of my hard-earned money."

Jim was understandably annoyed and angry with his dad. He had loved him but that was not enough to make the situation acceptable. His dad simply hadn't done any tax planning while he was alive.

Jim had accumulated a lot of share options with his employer and wanted to sell them to pay his dad's tax bill. The share price was at a historic low price and that put him off.

I convinced him that he stop being embarrassed about his money problem and tell his employer why he really wanted to sell the shares. You should have seen the huge grin on his face when he told them as it made him feel so much better. They offered him a short-term loan against his shareholding. Simple!

**Is it about £2 million?**

Now, if you think about Jim's legacy and you think it's about £2 million you will have misunderstood the story.

"Leaving a legacy for my children and grandchildren was important, sure," he said, "but the reality is I just want to be remembered, for goodness sake, as someone who really cared about them and this is one way of me showing it."

This is about him as a human being with deep emotions going on inside of him, just like everyone else. This is about wanting to be remembered by his grandchildren, who he adores and cares about too.

That's what's driving him – it's not the £2 million, it's not the legacy, it's Jim who wants to be remembered.

**Is it about Jim's need for extra income?**
"It's not about income," Jim told me. "It's about dreams. It is really hurting me that I have hidden and buried my dreams which are just festering away and will die with me. I was so busy in the office during my life that I completely forgot about them."

You see, Jim did a lot of business travel for around 40 years, busting a gut, providing for his family. But he never got to see the countries he visited. Just busy airports and bland office space and meeting after meeting after meeting.

**It's never about the money**
No, Jim's issue was not about the money or the tax, it was really about his love for his children and his desire to realise his buried dreams.

You see, it is never just about the money. Money, per se, does not matter. It's what money can do for you that does.

### *Meet Uncle Chacha-ji*

This is one of my family stories I tell my own three children, in the hope of teaching them something of value.

My father's brother, whom I call Chacha-ji (meaning 'young uncle'), never left his childhood home on the small farmstead in Punjab where he lived with my grandparents. He got married and had children but he never moved away from the family smallholding where they had cows, grew potatoes, corn, chillies, aubergines and sunflowers for oil. My grandparents owned several parcels of land in the village that they rented out too and were totally self-sufficient.

Uncle Chacha-ji was too lazy to find his own farm or run his own business and instead relied on my grandparents for everything. Their nagging flew straight past his ears without falling in. Uncle wanted an easy life.

In 1978, Bibi-Ji (my grandmother) passed away a couple of years after Baba-Ji (my grandfather). Do you think Uncle Chacha-ji pulled his socks up and set to take over the farm in their place? Of course not! He lived off the money his parents had made and when that ran out he started selling off the parcels of land.

Today, Chacha-ji lives with his wife on a tiny scrap of land in a shelter that is just 12 metres by 10. My father has given him a few cattle so he can at least survive. Chacha-ji is in his late 60s now. He has a long white beard and his clothes are ragged. His children rarely come home to visit.

Uncle Chacha-ji refused to listen to advice. He buried his head in the sand and would not face the future. He did not look at his financial landscape. He ran out of money and has nothing. Instead of growing his inheritance, he spent it.

What you leave behind matters. It matters hugely.

JOIN ME UNDER THE MAPLE TREE

1. As a sage in your wiser years, what financial advice would you give to a younger version of yourself at age 25?

______________________________________________

______________________________________________

2. How can you simplify your life further so that you can continue to enjoy your journey?

______________________________________________

______________________________________________

3. If you were directing the movie of your life, how would you want it to end?

______________________________________________

______________________________________________

4. What difference do you want to make through your giving and philanthropy?

______________________________________________

______________________________________________

______________________________________________

5. Why is that important to you?

______________________________________________

______________________________________________

______________________________________________

6. If you did not do that, what then?

______________________________________________

______________________________________________

______________________________________________

7. How do you want to be remembered?

______________________________________________

______________________________________________

______________________________________________

*"Four Seasons fill the measure of the year;*
*There are four seasons in the mind of man:*
*He has his lusty Spring, when fancy clear*
*Takes in all beauty with an easy span:*
*He has his Summer, when luxuriously*
*Spring's honey'd cud of youthful thought he loves*
*To ruminate, and by such dreaming high*
*Is nearest unto heaven: quiet coves*
*His soul has in its Autumn, when his wings*
*He furleth close; contented so to look*
*On mists in idleness—to let fair things*
*Pass by unheeded as a threshold brook.*
*He has his Winter too of pale misfeature,*
*Or else he would forego his mortal nature."*

*John Keats*

## What Are Your Freshest Thoughts?

## The Four Seasons Matrix

The Seasons of Nature, Life, Wealth and Financial Planning Aligned

| | **Seasons of Nature** | **Seasons of Life** | **Seasons of Wealth** | **Financial Planning** |
|---|---|---|---|---|
| | | **THE SEED** | | |
| **Pre-Spring** | Select seeds | Learn<br>Establish<br>Flourish | Good money habits | Three pots:<br>Spend<br>Save<br>Invest |
| | | **SPRING**<br>**PLANTING AND NURTURING** | | |
| **Mar.**<br>**Apr.**<br>**May** | Sow seeds<br>Fertilise<br>Water | Excitement<br>Optimism<br>Newness | Saving<br>First house<br>Starting a family | Pay-cut to save<br>Emergency fund<br>Mortgage<br>Pension |
| | | **SUMMER**<br>**GROWING AND WEEDING** | | |
| **June**<br>**July**<br>**Aug.** | Watering<br>Weeding<br>Blooming<br>Flourishing | Full of life<br>Buzzing energy<br>Playing/ Fun | Saving<br>Luxury spending<br>Career change<br>Bigger house<br>Educational costs | Keep it affordable<br>Develop a proper financial plan<br>Use Tax allowances<br>Set up Wills |

| | Seasons of Nature | Seasons of Life | Seasons of Wealth | Financial Planning |
|---|---|---|---|---|
| **AUTUMN**<br>**HARVESTING AND PREPARATION** | | | | |
| **Sept.**<br>**Oct.**<br>**Nov.** | Reaping<br>Ploughing<br>Cultivation<br>Some leaves fall to the ground | Freedom<br>Rewarded<br>Celebration<br>Savouring life<br>Gratitude<br>Fear | Spending<br>Bucket list<br>Save time/ tax<br>Generating income | Refine<br>Financial Plan<br>How much is enough?<br>Lifetime cash-flow<br>Review Wills |
| **WINTER**<br>**PREPARING FOR THE NEXT SPRING** | | | | |
| **Dec.**<br>**Jan.**<br>**Feb.** | Dormancy<br>Energy conservation<br>Hibernation<br>Leaf litter enriches the soil | Slowing down<br>Recuperation<br>Reflection<br>Peace of mind<br>Contentment | Preservation of capital and income.<br>Healthcare costs<br>Passing on financial legacy and non-financial legacy. | Estate planning<br>Inheritance<br>Tax Planning<br>Review Wills<br>Implement various Trusts<br>Lasting Powers of Attorney<br>Philanthropy |

# TIME TO WRITE

To make it easier for those loved ones left behind including executors, please let them know what you own and where it is kept by giving them a copy of these four pages.

The total value of unclaimed financial assets in the UK has not been accurately defined but it is approximately £15 billion to £20 billion, (Unclaimed Assets Register 2019).

## *Who are my key contacts?*

| | Name/Address | Contact |
|---|---|---|
| Power of Attorney: | | |
| Has EPA/LPA been registered? | | |
| Solicitor: | | |
| Accountant: | | |
| Chartered Financial Planner: | | |
| Tax Office: | | |

## *Your Will?*

| | |
|---|---|
| Original held with: | |
| It is dated: | |
| It was drawn up by: | |
| Is it up to date? | |
| Are you claiming the transferable residential nil-rate band? | |

If so, the following documents are needed for the spouse or civil partner who died first. Record the location of these documents:

| | |
|---|---|
| Copy of Grant of Representation | |
| Deed of variation or disclaimer executed in respect of property inherited from them | |
| Death Certificate | |
| Will | |

## *Bank & Building Society Accounts (including online accounts)*

| BANK/BUILDING SOCIETY (NAME, ADDRESS, BRANCH) | SORT CODE | ACCOUNT NO | CONTACT |
|---|---|---|---|
| | | | |

## *Credit cards and Loans*

| Name | Account no | Contact |
|---|---|---|
| | | |

## *My Assets*

| PROPERTY | Address | Approximate value |
|---|---|---|
| | | |

| Ownership | Outstanding Loan |
|---|---|
| | |

## *Other Property*

| PROPERTY | Address | Approximate value |
|---|---|---|
| | | |

| Ownership | Outstanding Loan |
|---|---|
| | |

| Comments and Notes |
|---|
| |

## *Policies*

| General Insurance | Life Insurance | Healthcare |
|---|---|---|
| | | |

## *Investments*

***(Investment bonds, unit trusts, ISAs, stocks and shares, pensions, premium bonds, national savings etc.)***

| Type | Plan or Account No | Value | Contact |
|---|---|---|---|
| | | | |

| Comments and Notes |
|---|
| |

## *Gifts Made During Lifetime*

| Date | Amount and/or Asset | Recipient |
|---|---|---|
| | | |

## *Gifts of Surplus Income*

| Tax Year in Which Made | Net Income | Net Expenditure | Surplus Income |
|---|---|---|---|
| | | | |

| Gifts Made | Beneficiary Contact Details |
|---|---|
| | |

## *Details of any Trusts*

| Name of Trust | Contact |
|---|---|
| | |

## *Digital Assets*

| Electronic Data | Passwords | Info |
| --- | --- | --- |
| | | |

## *Please use this section...*

| Additional Info where Items are Stored |
| --- |
| |

## *Other Info*

| | |
| --- | --- |
| Medical Research Bequests | |
| Where deeds are kept | |
| Safe boxes | |
| Details of organisations, clubs, subscriptions | |
| Utility Companies | |
| Plumber, electrician, cleaner, gardener | |
| Funeral Arrangements | |

# PART TWO

# BEYOND WEALTH

*“Then said a rich man, Speak to us of Giving.*
*And he answered:*
*You give but little when you give of your possessions.*
*It is when you give of yourself that you truly give.*
*For what are your possessions but things you keep and guard for fear you may need them tomorrow?”*

*Khalil Gibran*

# TRUE WEALTH

I have talked so far about achieving financial happiness and *meaning* in our lives. We all know that ‘money can’t buy’ us ‘happiness’.

In testing this out, I ask clients, “If I doubled your money would it double your happiness?” The response is usually a bit of a laugh followed by, “Of course not.”

Once you think you have acquired enough money to make sure you flourish and blossom in the Seasons of your Life you need balance in the other areas too.

## It’s Not About Money

Our worries and anxieties are, to a large extent, made up of fears surrounding money and/or politics. Existential fears – those about God, our own mortality and meaning – often remain, regardless of our financial standing.

***“Without a rich heart, wealth is an ugly beggar.”***

Ralph Waldo Emerson

This does not mean that you have to be financially wealthy. It has more to do with the reality of your life and your relationship with money. I know many millionaire clients who used to have more than enough but were unhappy and rarely experienced True Wealth. I know others who are not financially independent but are some of the happiest people I've ever had the pleasure to meet.

I find that people with less money are often wealthier. "How is that possible?" you may ask.

From my experience, True Wealth originates from a place of abundance. If you then add *meaning*, only then will you be truly alive. Once you start embracing gratitude and are no longer worried about anything else you can enjoy life to the fullest and share what you have with others. If you agree with this basic tenet then you can understand that you will be as wealthy as you feel, irrespective of how much money you have. I don't just believe, I *know*, that money cannot make you happy. Happiness is an internal mindset, not an amount measured by money and material things. Everybody is different and you cannot accurately measure happiness. It is a mindset you need to cultivate and grow.

At the age of four, my son Karam had plenty of toys and yet he always wanted more. This is human nature and he is only a child. I have seen adults, however, who measure their success in life in pounds and pence. How sad.

True Wealth is a much broader concept. Ask those in poor health whether they want more money or better health. "Your health is your wealth." My parents brought me up to believe that and it's true.

### *Money is freedom*

I would go a step further in saying that freedom is more important than money. It is better to live the kind of life you want than to earn more money and feel trapped by it. Don't sell your freedom.

## The Four Freedoms

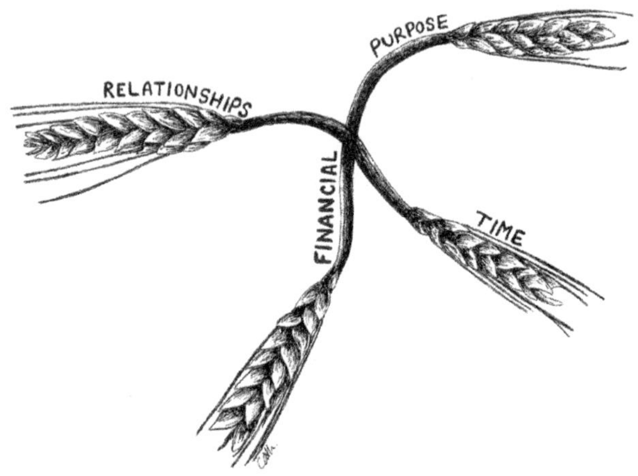


***"Freedom is what you do with what has been done to you."***

*Jean-Paul Sartre*

During my research with clients, I have learned there are four main types of freedom:

1. **Financial**
   To go to work because you want to and not because you need to.

2. **Purpose**
   To find more meaning and do purposeful work either paid or unpaid.
3. **Relationships**
   To spend more time with people in loving relationships, family, friends, work colleagues and in the community.
4. **Time**
   To be in complete control, not having to rush and keep ticking things off the To-Do or To-Get List.

***What can we learn from Nature here?***

Nature is active in all four of its Seasons. So too should we all try to have activity in all four areas listed above. With balance in all four areas, we can do what we want, when we want and with whom we want.

I remember taking my children to Trelissick Gardens, a National Trust park in Cornwall, for a nature walk and treasure hunt.

Amrit, my middle child, in particular, relished the challenge and was thrilled to have found a carpet of white snowdrops, their milky-white heads raised under the bare Winter trees. Snowdrops are so resilient they even bloom under a blanket of snow if they have to. Every year they are the first flowers to appear after a barren Winter and never fail to provide us with a boost of optimism and joy. What was really fascinating to me that day was that they each had six petals.

## *Six Paths to True Wealth*

Just as the snowdrop signals new life, growth and hope and has six petals, I believe there are six paths to True Wealth.

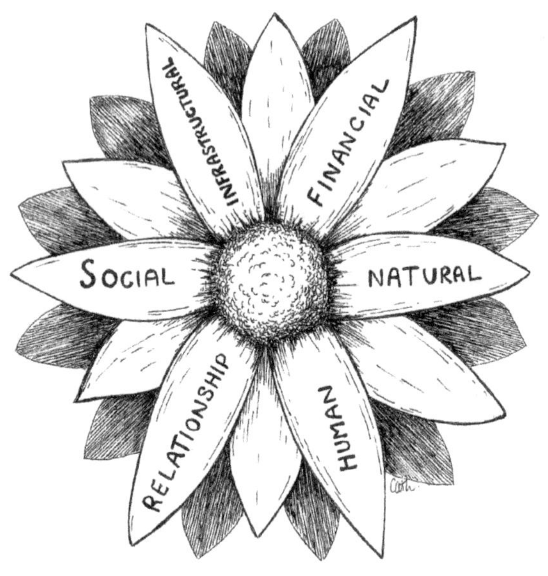


### #1 Financial wealth

Financial wealth means achieving financial independence and having the freedom to do whatever you want to do. If you do go to work then it is because you want to, not because you have to. The key to financial happiness is to make sure your wealth is in the right Season for you.

**#2 Natural wealth**
Natural wealth is about energy and Nature. It is also the environment around you. This is an important part of your life.

**#3 Relationship wealth**
Relationship wealth is all about having great, loving relationships with your family, friends and work colleagues. It is about having interests outside of work and it's about the lifestyle you live. These things add up.

**#4 Infrastructural wealth**
Infrastructural wealth is existing wealth tied up in tangible assets such as property, land and infrastructure. It is not traditional wealth.

**#5 Social wealth**
Social wealth is about where you live and work and the community to which you belong. Giving back and helping others shapes how rich our lives are.

**#6 Human wealth**
Human wealth is also made up of four parts. They are cultivated in the heart, mind and soul.

1. **Spiritual wealth**
   Knowing your true *meaning and purpose* in life. Knowing your *why*.

2. **Physical wealth**
   Being healthy and having the energy to perform tasks grants you wellness.

3. **Intellectual wealth**
   Having gifts and talents, knowledge and experience to master whatever you put your mind to.

4. **Emotional wealth**
   Having emotional intelligence and being aware of your emotions and of those around you.

## Learn From the Snowdrop

Now that you know the proper definition of True Wealth, it's great to know that you have the power to control each and every one of those six areas, paths, or petals.

You may believe you are already *rich* in many of

these areas, or maybe, like many, due to the *noise* of life, you have been taking many of them for granted.

Just as we know the importance of looking after Nature and we respect the tremendous job it does of looking after our planet, it is also our responsibility to look after ourselves and to restore our inner balance, our inner harmony.

Examine these six important paths to happiness with your heart not your head. Are you walking your talk? Are you truly taking steps down each of those paths? Congratulate yourself for the steps you have taken in some of the areas and know it is not too late to change and explore new paths.

It is only when we have balance in each area that we can develop the resilience we need to cope with the storms, shocks and curve balls that life can throw at us. It is only with this inner harmony that we can be hardy like the little snowdrop and flower year after year. It is only by treading all six paths that we can enjoy a rich life of True Wealth and happiness.

Early financial success is a poor teacher and I believe a good work ethic will get you far. Yet working too hard, which is a trap many of us fall into all too easily, means you are likely to sacrifice some of these petals in so doing. It is rare that I meet someone who has not placed work over happiness at some point during their journey.

Try to slow down and reflect every once in a while. Examine all six petals of the snowdrop of your life and do what you can not to sell yourself short in one or more areas.

When we have True Wealth, we feel more fulfilled thanks to operating from all six petals.

We can grow and manage them and teach our children and others and pass on these treasures for many generations.

## Human Nature is a Poor Investor

When it comes to investing money, experience has taught me that human nature is a poor investor. We can be our own worst enemies. Science calls this *behavioural finance*. It is critical, therefore, that you recognise this and learn to plan carefully and then stick to that plan. Earlier in this book I said that the key thing to getting comfortable is getting uncomfortable.

Humans can be irrational. They make expensive mistakes. They are frequently and understandably anxious about finance.

## The Four Sides to Human Nature

Understanding human nature here is key and I believe that there are four sides to us.

1. **Physiological**
   We are driven by fear. Some say that FEAR is an acronym for False Evidence Appearing Real. Instinct leads us to move away from danger. If we are faced with a lion in a jungle then this fear is there to save us. In the world of finance it can cause us to hijack ourselves.

2. **Psychological**
   If we have had a bad or deeply traumatic experience with money in the past, that emotion stays with us. Our minds put up barriers to protect us from feeling that bad again. We just don't want to go there. Studies have shown that losing money feels twice as bad as making money feels good. We've read the research. We are understandably wary.

3. **Intellectual**
   I don't want to say that many people are ignorant, but with all the emotion and fear surrounding it, it is easy to miss the point. Money is just a tool. While we should consider what it represents and what it can do for us and for others, most often we focus on the numbers. Unfortunately, we often forget about inflation. A first class stamp has tripled in cost during the last 20 years alone. Instead of focusing on the numbers we should focus on the purchasing power of our money. Money is not a currency. A farmer is not interested in the value of their land as that will go up and down. All they are interested in is whether their crops can be sold and their family fed.

4. **Cultural**
   We follow the herd. Investing is simple, or should be; we should buy low and sell high. However, when there is stress in the markets, or there has been a crash, we tend to sell out and mitigate further loss. The shrewd, however, realise that is usually the time to go and buy more while prices are low. This is another example of where we hijack ourselves. The Rockefeller family took advantage of this back in the 1930s by patiently buying stock that was being sold off by panicking individuals when prices had plummeted. In today's money the fortune they amassed would be worth over US$400 billion.

As a professional Chartered Financial Planner my responsibility is to make sure that I work with my clients to build and test a plan that manages human behaviour and allows my clients to achieve a balanced life as they aim for True Wealth. Without my help many would use too much concentrated fertiliser on their financial crops whenever their financial landscape looks likely to be destroyed. I am able to show them that the storm will pass and the sun will rise.

## What Are Your Freshest Thoughts?

JOIN ME UNDER THE MAPLE TREE

1. What is the connection between investment return on your wealth versus the return on your life?

____________________________________________

____________________________________________

____________________________________________

____________________________________________

2. How wealthy are you, based on these six petals?

____________________________________________

____________________________________________

____________________________________________

3. What can you improve on?

____________________________________________

____________________________________________

____________________________________________

____________________________________________

4. How can you do that?

____________________________________________

____________________________________________

____________________________________________

____________________________________________

5. To help you do that, who can you build accountability with?

____________________________________________

____________________________________________

____________________________________________

____________________________________________

## *Ambition*

***"Nature's heralds swirl in space,
their tunes hold beauty that I cannot touch.
The rainbow's arc spreads wide, beyond my grasp towards such promise
that my dreams, forever distant, fuel my heart's own song.
I will become great when the lark descends –
Or when I rise to greet the lark."***

*Jo Parfitt and Parminder Bains*

# SUCCESS TO SIGNIFICANCE

The rainbow is a metaphor for success; both temporary and shallow.

Imagine how it might feel if the *rainbow* were there all the time? What if it were as strong and sturdy as a majestic oak tree, rooted deep, standing tall, stretching towards the sky? If success were an oak tree, I could gaze at it for as long as I wanted.

Success is not an oak tree. It is a rainbow. It is a rainbow that keeps moving and disappearing and we know that when and if we do reach the end, the pot of gold will have moved again. And yet, it is the pursuit of the end of the rainbow that motivates us to strive and to keep moving forwards.

## We Have So Much to Learn

We are all on a journey. We are all a 'work in progress'. We learn most by doing and I know I have much more to do and much more wisdom to gain. It's the same for all of us, irrespective of the Seasons of Life in which we find ourselves.

When we are in the Spring and Summer Seasons of Lives our natural mindset lies in the hunter/gatherer mode of acquiring, getting, winning and achieving. Autumn is more about harvesting. Moving from Autumn to Winter is about releasing and relinquishing and it is during this period that we usually grow our inner strength. We do not tend to see this clearly at the start of the Spring Season of our Lives. This is normal.

## The Three Motivations

The intrinsic value my clients tell me I give them, besides solving financial problems and helping them grow, protect and pass on their wealth, is profoundly intangible. In the time that I spend with them, it always transpires that their issues are not about money at all. Instead, they are much more about the impact financial happiness has had on their lives and how it has made them feel.

I have learned three main things about my clients and what makes them do what they do; what drives them forever onwards:

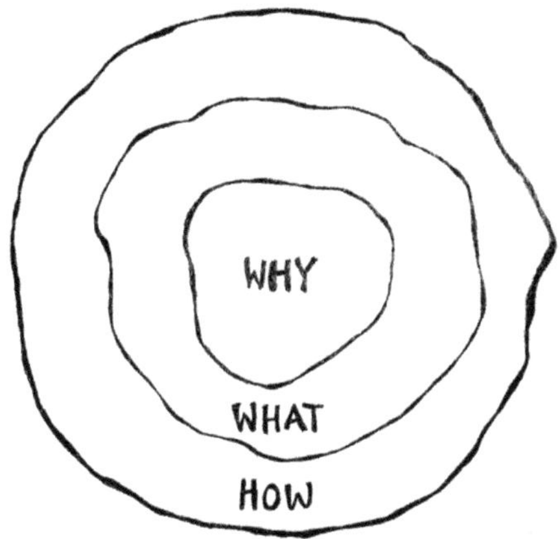


### *Their* WHY

They want me to make a difference in their lives so that they can live a life of True Wealth in which they enjoy all of the six petals of our snowdrop. Over time, they want to give vision to their wealth and make it meaningful in more than just monetary terms. They don't want their hard-earned money to be in vain. They want the effects of their money to have an impact on their lives and the people and causes they love, now, later and after their death. They want to make a significant difference. The *why* is what matters to them above all. This is their *why*.

### *Their* WHAT

The outcomes they really desire are *non-financial* and then *financial*, in that order. As we are all different, some want to preserve the rainforests, help fund a cure for cancer, whilst others want to let their grandson buy a house or ensure their spouse is taken care of should they no longer be around. The *what* is all about the specifics, the details of their *why*.

### *Their* HOW

By putting myself in their shoes and really understanding their lives, their biggest fears, aspirations, hopes, dreams and their financial landscape I am then, and only then, able to see which financial tools can make this happen. This is the *how*.

## Searching for Significance

If I had not had the courage to ask my clients the right questions their answers would have been superficial.

You can put metrics on wealth and measure it in various ways but it is impossible to measure intangibles such as peace of mind and a good night's sleep. I continually find in my client conversations that almost everyone battles with one major obstacle. This typically manifests in their mid-forties, the Summer Season, when their ambition peaks. Life takes a back seat as work takes over. We become increasingly hurried. Some of my clients tell me that deep down something is missing. Often they just can't put their finger on it.

**"Soon after a man turns 40 he is likely to tackle a huge undertaking. Something that appears to be slightly out of his reach."**

*Donald Joy, Professor in Human Development and Family Studies at Asbury Theological Seminary and author of* Men Under Construction

As we get older and attend more funerals we tend to become more aware of our own mortality. When all's said and done, our success is pretty empty unless it includes a corresponding degree of *significance.*

Too often, we fill our time with being a busy bee and cram our days with activities and tasks that give us no real joy.

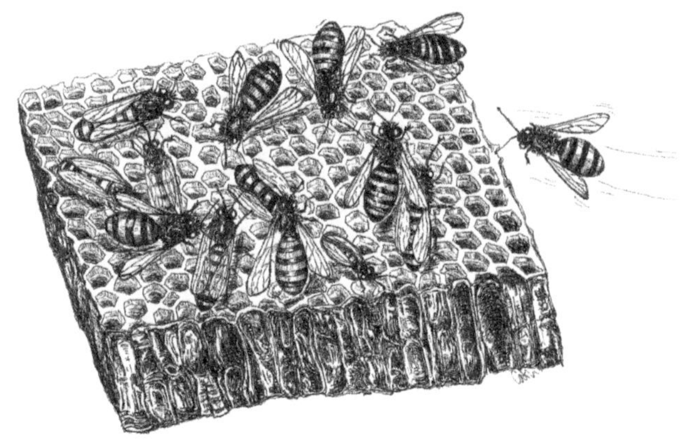

I used to be guilty of this and filled my days with making and spending money and getting involved in projects in and out of work. We distract ourselves with competition in business, sport and forming relationships. We know that we are not really happy and that something is missing. There must be more to life. However, we continue to pedal faster and faster on our proverbial hamster wheels, usually to justify abandoning them every once in a while and getting away from it all, drinking cocktails in the sunshine on a lovely warm, sandy beach. Before long, however, we are back at our desks, pedalling faster than ever.

The 'missing piece' is *meaning*. Clients tell me they want to do something more meaningful with their lives and find something that gives them a feeling of fulfilment and purpose. We all tend to pick up these signals but most people ignore them. They tell me, "I am just too busy right now. The time is not right."

## There Will Never Be a Right Time

In the Summer Season of our Lives it is often noisy and frenetic. We do not want to listen to that small whispering voice in our hearts. So, we keep running out of time and deafen this internal voice in the process.

We can barely remember what we did last Tuesday, never mind last October. We just want to prove to ourselves and others that we can accomplish something big. “At what cost?” I ask.

My clients usually tell me at this point that they feel trapped on this hamster wheel and beg me to help them get off it.

Almost everyone I have spoken to, both inside and outside of my professional life, has this realisation only to immediately sleepwalk back into their task-driven lives!

The Seasons are necessarily in a constant state of transition. I argue that we need to periodically shift our focus if we are to grow healthily during our different Seasons of Life. We have to learn to intuitively know when it is time to move on and realise as quickly as possible that we can only get and acquire so much. I know exactly what that feeling of emptiness is like when you find that pot of gold at the end of the rainbow... and then what?

Even when I show my clients that they have enough financial assets and enthusiastically shout, “Today’s the day!” they get all excited but then snuggle back down into the chocolate brown sofa in my office.

Ultimately, it is fear that stops them from taking action and making a change. Typically, they make all kinds of assumptions, often very believable, as to why they can’t stop buzzing around like busy bees and really live the dreams they tell me about and the life they know deep down that they really, really want.

## Why Do We Block Our Own Happiness?

Humans rarely change unless they have a profound life changing experience, like a near death experience or spiritual awakening.

Mine happened relatively early in my life and very early in my daughter Aman's life, when we thought we would lose her just after birth.

There is no need to wait for such a shock.

**"The important thing is not to stop questioning. Curiosity has its own reason for existence. One cannot help but be in awe when he contemplates the mysteries of eternity, of life, of the marvellous structure of reality. It is enough if one tries merely to comprehend a little of this mystery every day."**

*Albert Einstein*

## Today is The Day

Not everyone needs to have a wake-up call – facing death or a spiritual awakening – to suddenly decide to do something meaningful with their lives.

The good news is that there is a palatable *third way*. It involves taking the time to regularly ask yourself the right questions, to ponder, to reflect and contemplate. The key is to have some accountability, otherwise you may never enjoy the fruits of your hard-earned harvest.

Ask yourself the questions that really matter. You can't afford not to ask yourself meaningful questions. Only you can do that deep inner work. This takes courage and discipline, but before you know it, it will become a habit that will serve you as it has for others, including myself. I guarantee you.

This is where the fruit is on the tree of life. Right at the tip of a branch. Growth occurs in the zone of discomfort.

We have no time machine. The time is now. Today is the day.

Have the courage and faith in yourself.

**"I wish I'd had the courage to live a life true to myself, not the life others expected of me. I wish that I had let myself be happier. I wish I hadn't worked so hard."**

*Bronnie Ware, palliative nurse,*
The Top Five Regrets of the Dying

No one has ever said I wish I'd spent more time at the office, on the road, or on the farm. It is tragic to think that many of us will leave this earth with our music still playing inside of us and that some of the best songs are those that will remain unsung and die with us.

**"Spring has passed, Summer has gone and Winter is here and the song that I meant to sing remains unsung. I have spent my days stringing and unstringing my instrument."**

*Bengali poet, Rabindranath Tagore*

The perfect moment will never come if you don't carve the time out for it. The sooner you do this, the sooner you will truly start to live.

I firmly believe that we all have gifts and talents given to us at birth and that we need to uncover and use them to live a life of *significance.*

**"The tragedy of life is often not in our failure but rather in complacency; not in our doing too much, but rather in our doing too little; not our living above our ability, but rather in our living below our capacities."**

*Benjamin E. Mays*

## What is The *Meaning* of Life?

Quite simply, the purpose of life is to live life on purpose, with *purpose.*

I worked in the City of London for over 20 years and, like many others, I got lost in my work. I let it define me. The line between who I was and what I did got blurred. I was truly lost but did not want to admit it. I fooled myself in thinking that one day I would take the time out to think about it but there was still more I wanted to achieve first. I felt that empty feeling at the end of the rainbow when you discover the crock of gold has moved.

In order to learn from the successes of others and find out how they did it, I regularly travelled overseas to spend time at conferences. I would listen to some great talks and keynotes. I would fervently network in order to gain a better perspective and come home with pages of notes, business cards, audio programmes, videos and books.

I wanted to be successful just like them but knew deep down that something was missing. I wanted to find that *golden recipe*.

Then I had an A-ha! moment.

***The golden recipe***

As I saw it, there were two kinds of people. Either they were in the same camp as me; driven to find greater success but knowing deep down what was really missing was meaning and purpose in their lives – the *golden recipe*. Or, they were part of a very small minority of people who had found it and walked around with this sense of calm and quiet confidence, smiles plastered all over their faces. They had the X Factor. I call them *X Factor Folk*.

I could not explain it at the time but X Factor Folk just felt different to the others, like myself, who were in the herd camp. In the *herd* camp we were always asking ourselves: "How do we get or do this or that thing?"

Even as a child, I was always curious and would never follow the herd. They went one way; I went the other. I learned that the herd is usually wrong and headed for the exit, so I was quite disappointed to realise that I too was now following the herd!

I decided to seek out what this X Factor was over the next couple of years. What did X Factor Folk know that we in the herd did not?

It's so obvious and right in front of our faces but, as is often the case, we let ourselves get in the way.

These X Factor Folk had found their *why*, their *purpose* – and it was unique to every single one of them.

Once they became aware of their *why*, they then knew their *what*.

Finally, they worked on the *how*. The success they enjoyed was purely a by-product of their actions and not necessarily measured by money.

Like most of the planet, I had got the sequence wrong. I was pursuing the *what* without knowing what my *why* was. The *golden recipe* is to first find your *why* and only then can you begin to work on your *what*, and finally, your *how*.

Viktor Frankl was a concentration camp survivor and author of *Man's Search for Meaning.* In his book he quotes the German philosopher Friedrich Nietzsche:

**"He who has a why to live can bear almost any how."**

*Friedrich Nietzsche*

There I was again.

So had I done the impossible? Had I found the pot of gold at the end of the rainbow at last? But wait, there was that empty feeling again. How on earth was I going to find my *why*?

I knew what I had to do now. I felt energised but also scared. What if I never found out?

What if I did?

What if it wasn't there?

It was like standing at the edge of a cliff and peering down into the deep black valley of nothingness.

These are tough questions people have been asking themselves for the past six thousand years of recorded history.

This is a question that haunted me but, deep down, I trusted my gut feeling and intuition that there was an answer.

I had to face my fear. The chamber of your heart you fear to enter holds the riches you seek. Just as the sun rises and gains strength and courage throughout the day, you too must embark upon this remarkable journey.

## The Last Piece of the Puzzle

I was hopeful. The next A-ha! moment arrived as a revelation. I continued on my voyage of discovery by networking with X Factor Folk to find the key that unlocked their treasure chests.

I found that either they had had a defining life changing experience, and/or they had a mentor. A mentor who did not offer solutions but taught them how to find their own solutions for themselves so that they could, in turn, teach others.

**"Give a man a fish and you feed him for a day. Teach him how to fish and you feed him for a lifetime."**

*Chinese Proverb*

The search began to find the right mentor to give me fishing lessons.

After about three years, I finally found him. He was almost 30 years older than me and his name was David. Little did I know at the time that he would completely transform my life. I was an ordinary person who found himself on an extraordinary journey.

David had laser-sharp focus in one major area: **asking me really good questions and then really listening to me!**

I was still pedalling faster and faster on my hamster wheel and very disillusioned when I first met him.

"What does Nature do when it is stressed?" David asked me.

"It slows down," I said.

There it goes again – another A-ha! moment – a bit like, as one of my colleagues would say: "Being hit across the face with a wet fish!"

## Take Time to Think

I created the habit of regularly scheduling time in my calendar to do one thing and one thing only: taking time out to *think*.

Intuitively it feels wrong. In practice, it is what really creates time.

**"There is only one thing on which virtually everything else in our lives depends. This is the quality of our thinking. Most of us most of the day do not take time to think for ourselves, we are just too busy doing and doing."**

*Nancy Kline,* Time to Think

It is no wonder that Isaac Newton discovered gravity while he was sitting under a tree and an apple hit him on the head.

The famous inventor Thomas Edison was not famous for his fishing. He used to spend several hours a day just fishing. Somebody once said to him, "Why are you such a terrible fisherman?" and his reply was, "Because I have never used bait. When you fish without bait, people don't bother you and neither do the fish."

It was actually during one of these fishing activities he thought of using the bamboo fishing rod as a filter for the light bulb!

Carving out time to *think* soon became an ingrained habit for me. I even have a *Thinking Room* in my house, in which my children also come to just sit and think.

I created a similar thinking room for my clients in my office, in the heart of the frenetic City. It worked. It gave my clients the time to come off their hamster wheels and just think with me.

My mentor, David, then helped me to excavate my heart, mind and soul and examine my own personal anthropological journey. I babbled and babbled, realising the mind works best if it hears itself speak.

**"The unexamined life is not worth living."**

*Socrates*

Let your past serve you.

The next A-ha! moment happened shortly afterwards.

## How I Found my *Why*

I had always helped and served others in my local community in Wolverhampton. This included doing voluntary charitable work for Dr Barnardo's while I was still at school, to helping out at a local hospice on the weekend. I thrived through my involvement with the Cubs and Scouts. I continued doing voluntary work until I left school. But then, over time, I got lost at university and once again in the corporate world. I joined the herd.

However, during one of my trips to India, I became acutely aware of a problem that was widespread – blindness. Not just any type of blindness, but one that could be cured by the simple removal of an eye cataract. The procedure cost around £30, or the equivalent of saving 8p a day for a year.

My uncle Satnam, a proud hardworking farmer in Punjab, had had this problem for some time before I paid for his operation. I then paid for one of my aunties to have a similar procedure performed on her. It was amazing to see the impact this made on their lives and uplifted me when listening to their stories. In addition, this impacts everyone else that they come into contact with as they no longer need to be dependent on them.

Over the next three years I organised for everyone in the village to get treated, before starting on the surrounding villages. On one of these trips, in 2016, I brought my whole family along. It was heartbreaking and painful to see blind children begging. Nobody would help them. These children were of a similar age to my children. My daughter Amrit was in tears watching them. I knew at that moment, deep in my heart, I had to help them.

My wife, Satbir, told me I should take my children to the hospital when the patients had their bandages removed so they could experience what it was like for them to see again. What a great idea! This experience resonated profoundly with me, resurfacing as I stepped onto the plane to go home. The flight may have been four thousand two hundred miles but the longest journey is always from the heart to the head.

As Mark Twain wrote:

**"The two most important days in your life are the day you were born and the day you find out why."**

*Mark Twain*

I was privileged to have uncovered my *why* and had 'woken up'. I strongly believe that we all seek to experience this feeling of being alive and that we can only do this if we find true meaning and purpose in our lives.

**"For success, like happiness, cannot be pursued; it must ensue, and it only does so as the unintended side effect of one's personal dedication to a cause greater than oneself or as the by-product of one's surrender to a person other than oneself. Happiness must happen, and the same holds for success: you have to let it happen by not caring about it."**

*Viktor Frankl*

You cannot live a life of significance without helping others.

I want to light up the darkness of the blind in bringing light to one million people wherever they may be in the world. It is my life's mission.

**"Dream no small dreams for they have no power to move the hearts of men."**

*Goethe*

***Your dreams are always bigger than yourself***
Mostly dreams involve helping others, encouraging you to create wealth not for your own ends but for the greater good. Let me tell you exactly how I found and built my dream and then started to make it happen.

From helping one person see again in 2012, I plan to save the sight of a million people.

This is my lifetime mission and has become the catalyst that drives my business forward.

We are all on our own personal journeys. In some way, I believe that what we are seeking is also seeking us. My vision is like the sun, giving me warmth during the day, and the moon, giving me light at night. It does not make a difference what Season of Life you are in.

Patanjali, the Indian philosopher eloquently wrote:

**"When you are inspired by some great purpose, some extraordinary project, all your thoughts break their bonds: your mind transcends limitations, your consciousness expands in every direction and you find yourself in a new, great and wonderful world. Dormant forces, faculties and talents become alive, and you discover yourself to be a greater person by far than you ever dreamed yourself to be."**

*Patanjali*

Or, as George Bernard Shaw said:

**"This the true joy in life, the being used for a purpose recognised by yourself as a mighty one [...] the being a force of nature instead of a feverish, selfish little clod of ailments and grievances, complaining that the world will not devote itself to making you happy. [...] I want to be thoroughly used up when I die, for the harder I work, the more I live. I rejoice in life for its own sake. Life is no brief candle to me. It is a sort of splendid torch which I have got hold of for a moment, and I want to make it burn as brightly as possible before handing it on to future generations."**

*George Bernard Shaw*

In all my business planning, there is one sole metric, a kind of North Star, that drives what we do and that is the number of eyes we can save.

Now I knew my *why*, I moved on to my *what*.

## How I Found my *What*

What is it I want to do with the gifts and talents I have?

Considering how the lives of clients and those they care about had been improved through their work with me, I knew I wanted to continue doing this work in my professional life. That was the easy part. I now realise that I have been helping my clients find happiness by giving vision to their wealth for most of my professional life. I found this *heroic* as, like my why, it involved doing something bigger than myself.

I feel financial planning, when done well, is a uniquely positioned field where one can truly transform clients' lives and those they care about for generations to come. For me, living a life of *significance* begins with realising the impact I can have on the lives of my clients and others they care about.

**"Each man is a hero and an oracle to somebody."**

*Ralph Waldo Emerson*

I want to help give baby boomers vision to their wealth.

## How I Found my *How*

How do I make sure I'm doing a good job?

I make sure my clients' wealth is in accordance with its Season and that it will transform seamlessly as they transition through the respective Seasons of their Lives. By helping them build their own meaningful legacy, I will build my own of giving sight to others.

I am very privileged and blessed to have fascinating transformational conversations with them.

I have been mentoring a young business owner whom I met at a conference in California in 2017. He shared my vision. His business provides financial planning to ophthalmic surgeons in the US and he has worked with them to cure blindness – not in India, but in Tanzania.

We're exploring ways of working together to make our vision come true on a global scale, using technology to send out the message and we're now creating movement.

So, in short, here are four of the methods I am using to achieve my dream – my 'how'.

- I created a charitable foundation, The Seasons of Wealth Foundation, dedicated to providing free cataract operations worldwide.
- I give all sales proceeds from this book to The Seasons of Wealth Foundation.
- I redirect 10% of all of the profits of Seasons of Wealth Limited towards The Seasons of Wealth Foundation.
- I mentor others who share my vision.

## Creating my Season of *Significance*

What really sustained my transformation during this Season of moving from success to significance was the successful combination of who I am, what I do and why I do it. It is a path less well travelled by many, but the joys you get to experience are very satisfying.

It makes no difference if you're the leader of 10,000 employees or a parent leading your children. Being of service to others is a very personal thing and it means different things to different people. You must be patient.

I am reminded of Gandhi, one of the world's greatest leaders, who was followed by 200 million people. Like Gandhi, true satisfaction does not come in the achievement but in the effort. It's not about the numbers (in Gandhi's case, of followers).

It's about the *why*. But we need the numbers to make it happen.

I'd like to tell you about one last A-ha! moment in my journey.

There is a time and purpose for every Season of Nature, Life and Wealth and you may not be surprised to learn that there is a time for moving from Success to Significance and that is in the late Summer to early Autumn Seasons of Lives. This is the optimum time as you will have significant energy and time to find the resources to fulfil your *why*.

If you change the soil of a pot plant, cut back some of the dead wood, give it some fertiliser and move it somewhere where it might be a bit happier, perhaps where it might get more sun, what happens?

It flourishes because you have re-potted it. It is the same with us. To successfully transition from success to significance it is necessary for us to *re-pot* ourselves. To make a big change within ourselves. This requires some effort.

The strength of your vision will drive this for you. My vision was like a powerful magnet and I realised that if I were to *re-pot* myself, I would need to use some of this stoic grit.

**I realised there was a mismatch between the corporate world's *why* and mine and so, I decided to set up Seasons of Wealth.**

Once again, like nature, my interests and those of our clients are in perfect harmony.

**"The day came when the risk to remain tight in a bud was more painful than the risk it took to blossom."**

*Anaïs Nin*

As we have learnt from Nature, nothing happens overnight. Things take their time.

A Season of Significance is the one in which you find your *why*.

## Find Your Why With the Ikigai

A little while after I found my *why*, my mentor, David, showed me a graphic. The graphic was of a Japanese concept they call *ikigai* that was devised around a thousand years ago. Now it all made sense. It is what the Japanese call *ikigai*, meaning a reason for being. They believe that the source of your value in life makes it worthwhile and gives it that elusive *meaning*. It is not linked to your financial status.

**"Each individual's ikigai is personal to them and specific to their lives, values and beliefs. It reflects the inner self of an individual and expresses that faithfully, while simultaneously creating a mental state in which the individual feels at ease. Activities that allow one to feel ikigai are never forced on an individual; they are often spontaneous, and always undertaken willingly, giving the individual satisfaction and a sense of meaning to life."**

*N Nakanishi, Age and Ageing*

I now share this idea with clients struggling with the concept of defining their purpose.

The illustration clearly shows how your *why* can be found when the four circles of what you love, what you are good at, what the world needs and what you can be paid for intersect. The book, *Ikigai: The Japanese Secret to a Long and Happy Life* by Héctor García and Francesc Miralles, will tell you more about this.

Trying to find your reason for being requires you to dig deep but once you've found it, I can assure you, the result will be illuminating and energising.

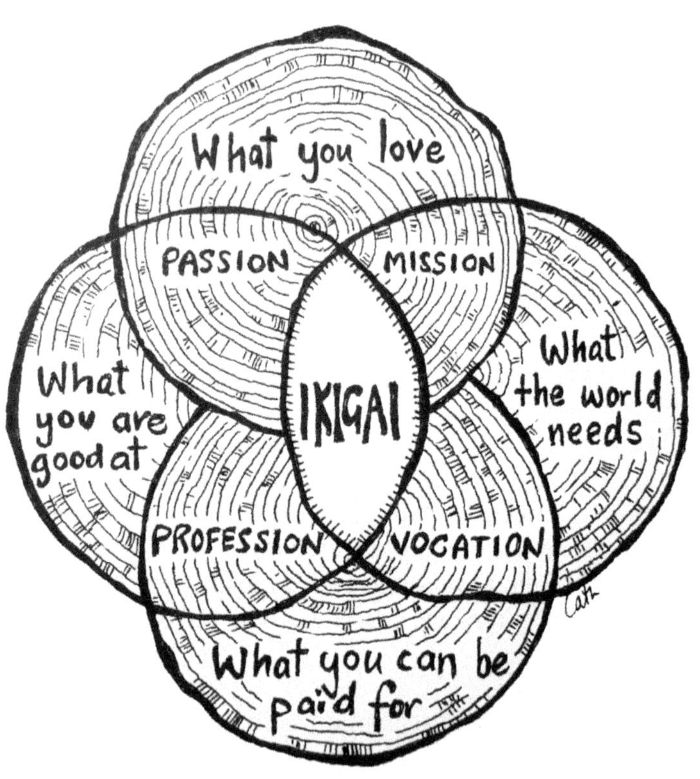
What you love
PASSION
MISSION
What you are good at
IKIGAI
What the world needs
PROFESSION
VOCATION
What you can be paid for
Cath

**"I believe that events in nature are controlled by a much stricter and more binding law than we suspect today...**

**"I believe in God, the God of Spinoza, who reveals himself in the orderly harmony of the universe...**

**"I believe that intelligence is manifested throughout Nature."**

*Albert Einstein*

Towards the end of his life, Einstein searched for an answer to the eternal question: What is our human purpose on this planet?

He then lent to this question the same quality of thought that led to his monumental theory of relativity.

He arrived at a very simple answer:

"We are here for others."

Deep down, we long to make a difference and ultimately, we will discover what really counts is how we made a difference to the lives of others. We all want to matter and that wisdom is as old as the hills.

In summary, I ask you to reflect on a quote from a man that gave the world something they did not think they needed:

**"Your time is limited, so don't waste it living someone else's life. Don't be trapped by dogma – which is living with the results of other people's thinking. Don't let the noise of other's opinions drown out your own inner voice. And most important, have the courage to follow your heart and intuition. They somehow already know what you truly want to become. Everything else is secondary."**

*That man was Steve Jobs.*

While success can be considered to be a rainbow, always out of reach, significance on the other hand is our oak tree. It is sturdy and well-rooted, grounded, it stands out against the landscape. Your significance – what you can make your money do for others – is what will make you stand out in the meaningful landscape of your life.

JOIN ME UNDER THE MAPLE TREE

1. Have you had a label given to you by the world that you do not like?

   ---

2. What do you lose in the process of all that gaining, winning and achieving?

   ---

3. What gifts and talents can you use in the Season of moving from success to significance?

   ---

4. Would you like the world to be a better place for your having been here and if so, what is your plan?

   ---

5. What would a life of significance look like to you?

   ---

6. What are you so passionate about that you would do it for free?

   ---

7. What do you really, really, really want?

   ---

8. How will you measure your life?

   ---

9. What do you want to be written on your epitaph?

   ---

*"Fame or integrity, which is more important? Money or happiness, which is valuable? Success or failure, which is more destructive?*

*If you look to others for fulfilment,*
*you will never be fulfilled.*
*If your happiness depends on money,*
*you will never be happy with yourself.*

*Be content with what you have;*
*rejoice in the way things are.*
*When you realise there is nothing lacking,*
*the whole world belongs to you."*

Lao Tzu, *Tao Te Ching*, The Timeless Guide to the Art of Living, *500 BC*

# IN THE END

The Seasons of Nature and the Seasons of Life are there to teach us lessons about ourselves, about others and about life. They are there to help us grow, to help us shape our characters and paint the blank canvas of all that we have yet to experience and for us to evolve as humans.

**"Life is like the seasons**
**After Winter comes the Spring**
**So I'll keep this smile awhile**
**And see what tomorrow brings."**

Cycles by *Gayle Caldwell,*
*sung by Frank Sinatra*

How true that is.

The Seasons of Nature and the Seasons of Life do not make an effort to change. Change simply happens and all we can do is stand back and observe its transformation.

Life and wealth are like the changing Seasons too and are inextricably linked. This law of Nature tells us that as the Seasons of your Life change, so too must your relationship with wealth, helping it to work in harmony with the corresponding Season of Wealth.

The Seasons of Wealth will not transform themselves; we have to create the change ourselves. The only way we can do this with any degree of success is by knowing the true purpose of our wealth.

Financial happiness is not an elusive butterfly; it is available to all who are determined to pursue it. The pursuit of financial happiness cannot be left to chance. We do not have the luxury during our Seasons of Life to wait for others to make prosperity *just happen for us*. We need to take action ourselves, which is why I wrote this book.

As you now know, your journey always starts by asking yourself the right questions.

We all need some tough love from time to time. That's why this book has not sugar-coated things. Hopefully, among the harsh realities and Uh-oh moments you have also found some A-ha! moments. This should help you start to remove some of the worries and anxieties you may already have. Do not be a leaf in a stream that gets carried along by the current.

## We are Human; We Have Control

Cultivate and design your own financial happiness today. I know of only two ways to climb the financial oak tree through the changing Seasons of Life: either you climb it or you sit on an acorn.

This book was written to help you climb that big old oak tree that is financial happiness. My stories are told to that end.

Financial happiness is not so much in having as sharing. We make a living by what we get but we make a life by what we give. Life is about giving not getting.

### *Pass on the story*

Life is a continuing story and the key to a fulfilling life lies in doing something with what you learn from this book and then in passing it on to someone else who will benefit from it. The person who won't read is no better off than the person who can't read.

### *Branch out*

In my experience, most people will wait until a perfect moment before making some significant financial decision that will transform their wealth and safeguard their financial future and happiness. Like I said, the fruit is always found at the end of the branch, so branch out, take a risk. Make a brave grab for the fruit. There will never be a right time – just do it. It is easy to bury our heads in the sand. It is easy to delude ourselves, thinking things have worked out fine until now, so why worry? It is vital that your Seasons of Wealth and Seasons of Life are in perfect alignment. If not, this can lead to financial suicide.

**"All problems become smaller if you don't dodge them but confront them. Touch a thistle timidly and it will prick you; grasp it boldly and its spines crumble."**

*Admiral William Halsey*

## What Next?

Financial happiness is a choice and just as farmers cultivate their fields by regularly weeding and fertilising the crops, so too you need to tend to your wealth by making sure you are handling it according to the right Season. Do not let it go under-nourished. Reasons come first and answers second. Your wealth must be protected from the storms that will inevitably arrive. As I began writing this during the Autumn of 2018, it had been exactly 10 years since the last recession, which was marked by the collapse of Lehman Brothers. Its nadir was reached in March 2009. There are always booms and busts in worldwide economies. It has happened before and it will happen again.

Recessions follow expansions. Last year the stock market crashed and things were the worst they had been in 10 years.

It's easy to worry about what might happen in the next 10 years. I, personally, have no idea. What I do know, though, is that we can all discover the treasures to be found in learning from Nature. The sage is not afraid of hoarfrost. Tomorrow's Spring will dawn anew.

One of the greatest lessons I believe our parents taught us, and one we should teach our children and grandchildren, is to take full responsibility for our actions.

I hope you find the courage to continually ask yourselves and sketch out your answers to the questions this book contains as they will help light the path towards financial happiness.

**"Whether you think you can or think you can't, you're right."**

*Henry Ford*

It's up to you.

Financial happiness, like the pot of gold at the end of the rainbow, is not a destination.

Enjoy the journey.

Parminder Bains
Summer 2019
*www.seasonsofwealth.co.uk*

# ACKNOWLEDGEMENTS

First of all, I thank you, the reader holding this in your hand. This is not your typical boring financial book! I hope this book takes you on an amazing journey of reflection and inspiration to take control of your future and lead and live a life of True Wealth.

I have been privileged to have met some really wonderful, amazing and insightful people on my journey so far. My parents taught me at a very young age to always ask for help and this has served me well. I will be eternally grateful for their wisdom and love.

I am forever grateful to the private clients in my professional life who have allowed me to conduct deep research with them over a period of four years, which has certainly opened my eyes and given me real depth of human nature. They have shared their life stories with me and granted permission for me to use them in this book.

Also my team, Tony and Marion, who have been very patient with me when I have been in my cave writing this book.

A special thanks goes out to my sweetheart, Satbir, and my three beautiful children, Aman, Amrit and Karam; you still get to teach me many more lessons. I have much to learn. Especially thank you for your extensive patience while I have babbled to you about seasons, nature, life and money. As my children would say: "Dad's gone off on one." It makes me laugh.

A lot of heartfelt thanks to Satbir for supporting me in the development of my ideas over the years and for letting me follow my dreams and having faith in me whilst managing a busy household. She truly has helped me live a life of No Regrets. You are my best friend and soul mate. The best is yet to come!

I also owe a great deal to my editor, Jo Parfitt, who has given me tough love over Skype, and also in person when I went to see her in Holland. She has helped me with my terrible grammar and past tenses. She brings decades of experience and also makes a great lasagne.

A lot of gratitude also to Cath Brew who did the fabulous drawings in this book to make it really come alive and for the layout and design.

I would also like to say thank you to the many delegates I have met around the world over the past eight years at international conferences who have been patient in listening to my many questions. There are far too many people to list here.

And so to David Scarlett, the most influential person I have met since my parents and my maths teacher, Mr Jones. Thank you for believing in me and helping me live fearlessly and for all the fun we have had and still do. Eating ice cream and walks in Ashdown Forest. For the amazing fishing lessons you have given me and for not being scared by my wild dreams. I really admire your love and compassion for others. You have become a trusted friend. Thank you for your continued guidance and inspiration.

Thank you to my uncle Satnam and his family in India. You helped show me the humility you have together with great wisdom. I am glad you took the courage to let me help you pay for your cataract operation because you were too embarrassed to ask for any help. This led me to much greater things.

Especially thank you to all the patients over the years whose eyes we have saved by funding free operations in North India. You have helped me to see what the true gift of sight is.

Thank you too, to God for inspiring me to help me find meaning and to leave the world a better place than when I first found it.

Parminder Bains

# ABOUT THE AUTHOR

Parminder S Bains is a Chartered Financial Planner and Certified Financial Planner who has been dedicated to Financial Planning since 1996. Since 2009 he has held both qualifications and was in fact one of the first in the UK to do so. A writer and speaker he has had articles published in the *Institute of Financial Planning magazine for financial planners* (now the Chartered Institute of Securities and Investments) and has achieved Top of The Table honours with an international organisation called MDRT. This represents the top half per cent of financial advisers in the world. He specialises in helping baby boomers give vision to their wealth and to pass on a meaningful legacy.

After working in the City of London with high net worth individuals for 23 years, in his early forties everything changed when he took his young family to India where they found themselves face to face with the tragedy of poor villagers living unnecessarily with blindness due to eye cataracts they could not afford to have removed. He decided there and then to turn his business on its head and start to use his gifts and talents for Financial Planning to work for the benefit of these unfortunate people. From now on Parminder pays close attention to making a difference.

A lifelong lover of the outdoors, particularly botanical gardens, he has always been fascinated by Nature and the changing Seasons. It did not take long for him to see that the Seasons were a strong metaphor for Financial Planning.

After years dedicated to major wealth management institutions and boutique financial firms he began to research what clients really wanted from a Chartered Financial Planner. He discovered that for most people their vision extended beyond making the most of their hard-earned money towards generating the kind of happiness and fulfilment that money can't buy. This, in turn, led him to set up a dramatically different business inspired by Nature and the Seasons which is called Seasons of Wealth. In addition, The Seasons of Wealth Foundation now supports eye cataract operations all over the world and aims to return sight to a million people.

One A-ha! moment has followed another and in 2016 he switched his City office with its view of a sea of skyscrapers and glass for a desk beneath a vast oil painting of the changing seasons. Out of his window he now watches a giant maple tree as it progresses through the Seasons from new buds in Spring to burgeoning with life each Summer, then to the magenta hues of Autumn followed by bare

Winter branches and to Spring once more.

An advocate of life planning, Parminder is committed to forging a radically new and complete family-focused approach to the financial planning process. Having invested heavily in his own education in self-mastery and coaching, he is qualified to guide and empower families to reach their potential through greater self-knowledge and understanding of their relationship with money. He firmly believes that having clarity about your life purpose is key to understanding how you should use your wealth, not only during your lifetime but also in passing on a meaningful legacy that will live on well beyond your passing. It's about life not just about money.

Now living in leafy Buckinghamshire, he enjoys spending quality time with his wife, Satbir, and their three beautiful children, Aman, Amrit and Karam. He is determined their children save a proportion of their income for giving to others.

To relax, he is a keen golfer and enjoys time to think while jogging in his local forest.

## The Hummingbird

The hummingbird represents to me anything that people think can't be done. It's usually linked emotionally to fear. It's all in our heads!

It could be via the power of coaching, having the courage and grit to leave their miserable employer and set up their own business, finding meaning and fulfilment or purpose.

It could be giving sight to one million people.

The hummingbird is doing what others think is impossible.

It is tiny and versatile and the smallest weighs less than a 1 pence coin.

Its wings can beat up to 200 times per second and its heart 20 times a second.

It can rotate in a complete circle allowing it to hover in mid-air, fly backwards, forwards, up, down, sideways and even upside down!

The laws of physics say it is impossible for it to do this...

Clearly nobody told the hummingbird!

# FURTHER READING


*Ikigai: The Japanese Secret to a Long and Happy Life*, Héctor García and Francesc Miralles, Penguin, 2017

*The Top Five Regrets of the Dying*, Bronnie Ware, Hay House, 2012

*Man's Search For Meaning*, Viktor Frankl, Beacon, 2006

*Men Under Construction*, Donald Joy, Evangelical Publishing House, 1993

*The Flight of the Soul Millionaire*, David Scarlett, Springtime Books, 2019

*The Hero With a Thousand Faces*, Joseph Campbell, New World Library, 1949

*Time to Think*, Nancy Kline, Cassell, 2015

*The Golden Ghetto*, Jessie H O'Neill, Affluenza Project, 1997

Lightning Source UK Ltd.
Milton Keynes UK
UKHW020805040620
364383UK00009B/638